WHAT IS THE SINGLE GREATEST ATTRIBUTE OF AN EFFECTIVE BUSINESS LEADER?

The answer is simple: listening—the ability to tune in to the needs and objectives of clients, customers, and colleagues. It is the single skill that Lee Iacocca believes can make "the difference between a mediocre company and a great company." It is the facility about which Mark McCormack says "in selling, there is no greater asset." It is also one of the most underrated and neglected tools of management.

Effective listening means tapping into the vast resources available to you, tuning in to the flow of information that can make you a better manager, a more effective employer, and a truly successful entrepreneur.

—Kevin J. Murphy
from *Effective Listening*

EFFECTIVE LISTENING

Hearing What People Say and Making It Work for You

Kevin J. Murphy

BANTAM BOOKS

TORONTO · NEW YORK · LONDON · SYDNEY · AUCKLAND

To all my friends and associates, who encouraged me to pursue a book on listening, and especially to Dick Sapir, Barbara Alpert, and everyone at Bantam Books for helping to make this book a reality.

EFFECTIVE LISTENING
A Bantam Book

Bantam hardcover edition / June 1987
3 printings through October 1987
Bantam paperback edition / January 1989

Library of Congress Cataloging-in-Publication Data

Murphy, Kevin J.
    Effective listening.

    1. Communications in management.   2. Listening.
I. Title.
HD30.3.M87 1987   658.4'52   86-47893
ISBN 0-553-27030-3

Published simultaneously in the United States and Canada

---

*Bantam Books are published by Bantam Books, a division
of Bantam Doubleday Dell Publishing Group, Inc. Its trademark, consisting of the words "Bantam Books" and the
portrayal of a rooster, is Registered in U.S. Patent and
Trademark Office and in other countries. Marca Registrada.
Bantam Books, 666 Fifth Avenue, New York, New York 10103.*

PRINTED IN THE UNITED STATES OF AMERICA

O   0 9 8 7 6 5 4 3 2 1

Dedicated to my father, Arthur Murphy, who taught me that ethics and family come first.

To my wife, Dolores, and my children, Kevin, Christina, and Kerri, for listening and supporting me during the preparation of EFFECTIVE LISTENING.

CONTENTS

INTRODUCTION

What is the single greatest attribute of an effective business leader? Is it the years of experience? Intelligence? Organizational skills? The answer is simple: The most successful leaders and managers *LISTEN*.

Listening—the ability to tune into the needs and objectives of clients, customers, and colleagues. It is the single skill that Lee Iacocca believes can make "the difference between a mediocre company and a good company"; it is the facility of which Mark McCormack, author of *What They Don't Teach You At Harvard Business School*, has said, ". . . in selling, of course, there is probably no greater asset"; it is the basis of the marketing breakthrough that made the Ford Taurus, a car built to the specifications of customers, employees, engineers, and dealers, one of the most successful automobiles since the Mustang; and sadly, it is one of the most underrated and neglected tools of management.

We've all heard the old saying, "What you don't know can't hurt you." Yet, every day, in factories, service facilities, and offices across the country, a manager's experience proves that proverb wrong. Raised on a steady diet of marketing courses, seminars in organizational behavior, sales management training, and classes in personnel management, managers still must face their futures without the single most important skill that will enable them to use their business educations—the ability to listen. And what they don't know *does* hurt them—by stifling

1

creativity, by encouraging them to talk when they should be tuning in, by undermining the communication process.

Hearing your way to success means discovering the many ways what you *do* know can help you. Effective listening means tapping into the vast resources available to you, tuning in to the flow of information that can make you a better manager, a more effective employer, and a truly successful entrepreneur, just as it did one satisfied client of mine.

All I knew about Jordan was that he was the owner of a well-diversified business, a self-made success whose desire to achieve had attracted him to my listening program. Because I wanted to open lines of communication with him before our initial meeting scheduled for late the following Monday morning, I sent him a copy of my self-published guide to effective listening on Friday.

I have had the pleasure of meeting many managers, but never before had I been greeted with such warmth. "You don't have to say another word, Kevin," said Jordan. "You've sold me on effective listening already." I was delighted; my book had won me a convert! Little did I know, however, that in nearly the time it took this creative entrepreneur to read it, he had turned my potentially profitable volume into a solid financial windfall.

Weeks before, a group of investors had expressed interest in a small division that Jordan was willing to sell. Over the weekend while reading my book, the entrepreneur had decided on his price, $3,000,000, and he began to formulate the arguments that he felt would be needed to obtain it.

Yet, early that Monday morning, as Jordan and the prospective buyers settled in around the conference table, something kept him from announcing his price; the "something" was a phrase he recalled from my book: "The better you listen, the more you learn about how the customer feels about your product." Right then and there, Jordan decided to give that advice a try. Instead of making demands, justifications, and excuses, he pressed his lips together and listened.

The investors were only too willing to fill the unsettling silence; they immediately launched into an extended rundown of the company's strengths and weaknesses, which culminated in the following offer: "We'll give you three and a half million and not a penny more." Sensing that his silence had put him in a position of strength and tuning in to the buyers' enthusiasm, Jordan accepted their offer, as a bargaining point. Less than an hour later, Jordan was shaking hands on a price of $3,650,000. "You don't always get what you pay for," Jordan said later with a laugh. "Your book was free. But it made me a $650,000 profit."

Actually, Jordan *had* made an investment: he had invested his time, effort, and even a part of his ego to make his buyers feel important, to encourage them to come forth with their ideas, and to *listen* for the signals he wanted to hear. And his investment didn't stop there, for Jordan carried the principles of effective listening into his organization as well, where his new skills are still paying off in higher productivity, better group morale, and increased accountability.

Going With the Flow. No matter what your industry, no matter what the objectives of your department, every working day is an eight-hour flow of information. If you ignore the constant exchange of information available to you as a manager, you pass up an opportunity to tune in to departmental problems, to decipher an employee's signals, and, in short, to make your department the best it can be. But put the single greatest attribute of the most successful business leaders to work for you, and you tap into an endless supply of ideas, suggestions, and solutions, empower yourself to select and hire efficient, creative employees, encourage team spirit, and increase morale and responsibility.

The Better You Listen, the Luckier You Get. My clients swear by it; Jordan banked on it; and Lee Iacocca built a dream on it.

Effective listening is, in truth, just one way to get to the top. Experience, a good track record, even simply being at the right place at the right time; any of these factors can propel you to the pinnacle of your profession— but only effective listening can *keep* you there. Aren't you ready to get lucky, too?

Part I

ARE YOU LISTENING?

Are You a Good Listener?

Answer yes or no:

1. When a problem arises at work, do you often react before gathering all of the facts?

2. After you receive the answer to a question and the other party starts talking about an unrelated subject, do you lose interest?

3. Do you have a tendency to daydream at a meeting after you have made your statement or completed your presentation?

4. Do you often finish statements for the slow, deliberate talker in the interest of saving time?

5. Do you view listening to an employee's personal anecdote as more of a waste of time than an opportunity to gain insight into his or her personality?

6. Do you feel uncomfortable asking employees if they understand your instructions?

7. If you received word that a layoff was imminent, would it preoccupy your thoughts during subsequent discussions with subordinates for the remainder of the day?

IT OFTEN SHOWS
A FINE COMMAND
OF THE LANGUAGE
TO SAY NOTHING.

ARE YOU A GOOD LISTENER?
ASK YOUR PEERS,
SUBORDINATES, SPOUSE,
OR CHILDREN.

8. When a customer or client is confusing you, are you hesitant to ask clarifying questions?

9. Do you become nervous or apprehensive in the presence of the top executive in your company?

10. Are you a good listener?

If you answered yes to *any* of the first nine questions, your natural tendencies are inhibiting your ability to listen under the pressure of day-to-day activities. This book will increase your awareness, sharpen your listening skills, and improve your performance all the way to the top.

If you answered no to all of the first nine questions and are not the chief executive officer of your company by now, you should either inform the company's owner of your nearly superhuman abilities or take a polygraph test. Anxiety, preoccupation, and pressure can undermine the abilities of even the best "natural listener." Open your mind and take the quiz again. Remember, what you don't know can hurt you, but what you *do* know can only help you.

To better understand the makeup of the effective listener, I administered this quiz to twenty top managers, all business leaders whom I had known to be truly tuned in to their employees' needs and goals. Most of them answered yes to at least four of the nine questions. To test the managers' objectivity, I asked one peer of each manager to complete the test *for* that manager; again, four of the nine questions were answered affirmatively, confirming the accuracy of the managers' self-assessments.

What about question 10: Are you a good listener?

More than seventy-five percent of the good listeners I surveyed answered no. Why? Because the better you listen, the more you learn about how little you know. Being a good listener requires that you remain aware of how poor a listener you can be when the heat is on.

If you answered yes to number 10, I suggest that you ask a peer, subordinate, your spouse, or your children to take the quiz for you; then brace yourself for the results. In so doing, you will have answered what could be question 11: Do you want to be a more effective listener? Your willingness to open yourself up to the scrutiny of others proves that you do.

1

What Is Listening?

• Listening is the accurate perception of what is being communicated. It is the art of separating fact from statement, innuendo, and accusation.

• Listening is a process in perpetual motion. It begins when one hears or observes what is being said, continues as one stores and correlates the information, then begins again with one's reaction.

• Listening is not the simple ability to decode information; it is a two-way exchange in which both parties involved must always be receptive to the thoughts, ideas, and emotions of the other. To be an effective listener, one must not only open the lines of communication and relax; one must compel others to do the same.

What else is listening?

• Listening is a natural process that goes against human nature.

LISTENING IS THE
ACCURATE PERCEPTION
OF WHAT IS
BEING COMMUNICATED.

2

Deterrents to the Listening Process

Communication Cancelled Due to Lack of Interest. From the first moment the speaker took his place at the dais, I knew that this man was someone I had to speak to face-to-face. His poise was remarkable; his message—on sharpening communication skills—was electrifying.

But as soon as I introduced myself to this self-professed "listening colleague," he launched into a monologue on his background, qualifications, and successes. I felt my eyes glaze over and my attention start to wander. Moments later, I "came to," embarrassed for my end of the communication failure.

"I'm sorry," I offered. "I didn't catch that last sentence."

"Oh, uh, right," he stammered. "What *was* I saying? Well, it couldn't have been important."

The Ego: The Basic Communication Block. Human nature is responsible for the most basic block to effective listening. By providing each of us with an enormous need to be *heard*, our egos overwhelm any desire to *hear*. The

AN OPEN MIND IS THE KEY
TO COMMUNICATION.

DON'T LET THE LINES OF
COMMUNICATION GET TANGLED
UP IN YOUR NEED TO TALK
TOO MUCH, TOO OFTEN.

result is a conversational stalemate: The listener loses interest in the speaker and the speaker, eventually, loses interest in the sound of his or her own voice.

To Whom Are You Listening?
A Manager's Quiz

Answer yes or no:

1. Do you discover only after good employees leave the company that they were unhappy or unchallenged in their work?

2. Do you often find out that a key account is lost only after reading the report a month later?

3. Does completing a budget or monthly report take precedence over addressing an employee or market problem?

4. Do you sense your subordinates are afraid to discuss sensitive matters openly with you for fear of reprisals?

5. Do you have a tendency to shy away from personnel problems in hopes that they will disappear?

6. Are you hesitant to institute change in your department?

7. Do you find it difficult to tell a subordinate that his or her performance does not measure up to your standards?

8. Do you find it difficult to terminate an employee even if the cause is more than justified?

When You Are Unable to Listen to Others, Chances Are It's Because You Are Too Busy Listening to Yourself. If you answered yes to any of the questions in the manager's quiz, your natural tendency to listen to your own thoughts, fears, and words is interfering with your need to listen effectively to others.

Our listening deterrents are our egos' defense systems. They are as natural, and as individual, to each of us as our fingerprints. Because you must tune in to your own listening blocks before you can open the lines of communication, you must identify which of the following listening blocks are distancing you from your subordinates and peers:

• The inability to relax and concentrate at the moment at hand.

• Preconceived ideas and thoughts.

• Talking too much, too often.

• Thinking of responses during the communication process.

• Lack of interest in the conversation.

If you answered yes to question 1 or 2, you aren't listening to your employees' needs. Your lines of communication may be tangled up in your tendency to talk too much, too often. If you answered affirmatively to question 3, your lack of interest is showing! Cultivate a feeling of reciprocity in your department or you may soon find yourself the managerial quarterback of a one-person team. A yes on question 4 or 5 may signal an inability to relax, to let your guard down with subordinates; while a positive answer to number 6 may indicate that your negative preconceived ideas are keeping you from changing to suit company needs. Finally, if you answered yes to question 7 or 8, you may be so concerned with an employee's possible response to a suggestion or reprimand that you may have abdicated your role as a guide to your subordinates.

THE INABILITY TO RELAX: LISTENING TO YOUR STRESS

When what's between your ears becomes a direct block to any external message that tries to penetrate them, it's impossible to listen effectively to others. Learn to take listening easy and listening will come easy; listen too hard to your own preoccupations, obsessions, and apprehensions, and your communication with your subordinates may come too little, too late.

The Preoccupied Manager: Great Caesar's Ghost. Physically, he's present and accounted for, but mentally he's just not all there. The preoccupied manager may be an organizational genius or a motivational whiz, but when his mind wanders away from the moment at hand, his skills are bound to follow.

The Message Is Transparent. The eerie presence at the desk may be too lost in thought to listen, but that doesn't mean she stops communicating. Subordinates can see right through the preoccupied manager—and straight to the heart of her message: "I'm not here for you." It is at that moment that the manager becomes little more than a haunting memory, and also at that moment that her people, for better or worse, begin to function without her.

Preoccupation: The Pitfall of the Conscientious Manager. Every manager, whether good, bad, or indifferent, is a *doer* by nature. Although the most effective manager has honed his or her ability to take appropriate action at an appropriate time to solve a specific problem in the workplace, even an ineffective manager is compelled to act, unfortunately, often before thinking. But when a manager

WHEN YOUR MIND WANDERS
AWAY FROM THE MOMENT
AT HAND, YOUR MANAGEMENT
SKILLS ARE BOUND TO FOLLOW.

ONLY WHEN YOU
STOP THINKING ABOUT WHAT
YOU CAN'T DO WILL YOU
BEGIN TO DO WHAT YOU CAN.

obsesses about his or her inability to take action when no appropriate action can be taken, preoccupation is the result.

Pre-empting Preoccupation. This means always being at the right place at the right time, physically and mentally. When personal concerns or business problems are stealing your presence away from the moment at hand, take a moment to focus on the here and now by asking yourself the following questions:

• Has this problem ever concerned me before? If so, did worrying about it help to solve it?

• Is the situation at this moment beyond my control? Is there anything I can do about it right now?

• When will a more appropriate time to address the problem arise?

And last but not least, look at your desk and ask yourself:

• Is there a current business concern more appropriate to the time and place that I can effectively deal with now?

Remember: Only when you stop thinking about what you can't do will you begin to do what you can.

The Intense Manager: Listening to Your Goals. So what's wrong with really tuning in to your objectives? Focus your attention too intensely on your goals and you overlook the one resource most likely to help you reach them—your people.

The Long-Range Problems with Shortsighted Goals. Laura was a top-notch performer, a sales manager who had catapulted her department at a small, one-product elec-

DEVELOPING A ROUTINE WILL
HELP RELIEVE THE STRESS
OF HAVING TO REMEMBER.

tronics company into industrywide recognition. It was no surprise to me, then, when she was recruited by a well-known national chain.

Yet, as soon as Laura took the helm, sales dropped; her reps, although able to write thousands of dollars in sales for the concern's main product line, suddenly seemed unable to move any of the ancillary products. Soon the VP of marketing had taken enough of an interest to begin sitting in on Laura's departmental meetings.

Laura was still a strong performer, and although her responsibilities had changed, her goals had not: experienced at one-product selling, moving her company's main line had remained her objective. This narrow focus had tuned out the importance of pitching ancillaries—and her intensity had frightened her subordinates, who knew better, into uneasy compliance.

The High-Intensity Lines. When the only lines of communication in your department are high intensity, what can the manager expect to hear? No static—but no input; no dissension—but no creativity.

The high intensity lines may seem to be the shortest route to your goals because they bypass the goals of your employees, but you'll never make the connection without them.

Keep your goals broad enough to encompass every member of your department and you'll foster a team spirit; set the limits of your personal goals within the bounds of your group objectives and your subordinates will see to it that you reach them.

Finally, replace the high-intensity lines with open lines of communication by using these awareness-building tools daily:

• *Develop a routine* and make communication time an integral part of it. Set your intensity aside and consider the scope of your responsibilities; then realistically schedule each of those duties into your daily planner. Use the hours between eight and nine A.M. and five and six P.M. to deal with the mechanics of your job—report writing, signing invoices, planning—so that you will be available during normal business hours for working and communicating with employees. Your subordinates will become partners in your goals, not adversaries to them.

• *Make notes*. Intensity does not "punch out" at the end of a day. Your single-minded devotion to your work can become a double burden: in the office it can be your biggest block to your ability to listen; take it home and it will overcome your awareness of your family.

Put your daily goals to rest by putting them down on paper. This simple action relieves you of the responsibility to commit your objectives to memory and to remind yourself of them hour after hour, day after day. Free your mind to relax and you free your ability to listen, both in the workplace and at home.

The Apprehensive Manager: Listening to Fear. Just what is the apprehensive manager afraid of? Ask him—he'll tell you that he doesn't know. Is he hedging? Absolutely not; *not knowing* is exactly what he fears most.

Past Imperfect, Present Tense. Recent studies have indicated that we, as human beings, spend more than sixty percent of our time obsessing about a future that has yet to arrive, another twenty percent rehashing a past that is beyond reclamation, and only the remaining twenty percent dealing with present concerns. With every man, woman, and child on earth devoting eighty percent of their energies worrying about situations that have already occurred or may never occur, is it any wonder that a manager's fear of the unknown can become one of his or her biggest blocks to effective listening?

The Uncertain Future. Although the apprehensive manager is, by virtue of his position, an agent of change,

change is often the very source of his anxiety. Times may change, affecting the economy; his company may change with the times, affecting his status; and if his status changes, how will his personal life be affected?

Short-term apprehension is a normal part of life; it is nothing more than a signal that you are reacting to the pressures and stresses of your responsibilities. But when apprehension becomes an obsession, when it becomes an automatic reaction to *any* stimuli, it can also become a twenty-four-hour-a-day block to your ability to absorb and assimilate information.

"Stress—Pass It On." This is the message an apprehensive manager communicates to his subordinates—and to anyone else who must come in contact with him or his department. And walking into it is like walking into a wall.

I began my consultancy as usual—by touring each department of the large food-processing plant with the individual managers. I found Jacob standing outside the doorway of the inventory control room, staring at the floor. When I approached, he extended one clammy hand, mumbled his name, then led me through the door.

But if the manager's manner was just the tip of the iceberg, the rest of the department was the glacier. As soon as we approached each station, the employees turned away; no greetings were exchanged, no questions asked, no introductions made.

Later, I asked Jacob for a rundown on his departmental problems. "No problems here," he answered, avoiding eye contact. "Do the employees express an interest in any time-saving technologies—computers, perhaps?" "They *don't*," replied Jacob, with enough emphasis to let me know that they didn't dare. He offered his hand. "If there's anything else, please let me know."

But there wouldn't be—I had learned more by listening to his apprehension echo throughout the department than he could ever tell me.

SHORT-TERM APPREHENSION IS
NOTHING MORE THAN A SIGNAL
THAT YOU ARE REACTING TO THE
STRESSES AND PRESSURES OF
YOUR RESPONSIBILITIES.

OFTEN, OUR INABILITY
TO RELAX MAKES
OTHERS NERVOUS.

Overcoming Communicative Dis-Ease. Often, our inability to relax makes others nervous as well. Although our apprehensions about establishing an open dialogue can be as obvious as a need to intimidate or as subtle as a stammer, they communicate with the same impact, and cause others to react in kind.

When apprehension keeps you at arm's length from your subordinates, it distances you from your goals as well. Although none of these exercises can eliminate fear, they will help you to overcome it—freeing you to absorb and correlate the communication you've been missing.

Fear: The Common Enemy. Leaders do not become heroes because they are without fear; leaders become heroes because they overcome fear. Just as you are apprehensive, so are your peers and subordinates. Recognizing fear as the common enemy will enable you to treat others as you would be treated, to draw them out gently, without pressure or intimidation. Make your common fear a common bond, and communication will flow.

The Worst Case Scenario. One manager passed along this insight on "thinking the unthinkable":

> Rumors were flying about the takeover of my company for months before the deal was announced, and, frankly, there came a point in time when my fears about my job security were keeping me from doing my job—which was even *worse* for my job security, now that I think about it. For weeks on end I worried about what *might* happen, until the day I finally sat myself down and thought the unthinkable. What was the worst that *could* happen? I could lose my job. And what if I did? I'd gotten this one, hadn't I? My morale improved by one hundred percent—and I'm still employed at the same company.

A MANAGER WITH
PRECONCEIVED IDEAS
WILL SOON HAVE
NO IDEAS AT ALL.

YOU MAY HAVE PLAYED
THE GAME BEFORE,
BUT MAKE SURE
THE RULES HAVEN'T CHANGED.

No one can battle the unknown—but make the enemy a known quantity and your nameless fear becomes a challenge. (By the way, research studies have indicated that fifty percent of employees who are outplaced due to organizational changes find more responsible, higher-paying jobs in a new company. That's the *realistic* worst case scenario!)

Breaking the Intimidation Chain. If *your* superior manages by intimidation, he or she is every bit as uptight, insecure, and nervous as you. Although that may seem like cold comfort to someone who must deal with the office bully, your listening skills and your new sense of awareness will soon give you the upper hand. Intimidation is a short-run phenomenon that is eventually overcome by a person's education and awareness of a situation. The apprehensions of your boss are blocking his or her ability to learn; yours are not.

PRECONCEIVED IDEAS AND THOUGHTS: LISTENING TO YOUR EGO

For more than two years I supervised a group of skilled electricians, machinists, and welders. Although I had little or no knowledge of the specifics of their jobs, we all recognized my limitations and operated on the following basis: I would provide the tools and equipment they needed, and they would work to the best of their abilities.

Within weeks, accountability and morale boomed. Our brief daily meetings to discuss both objectives and objections became a forum where my workers not only took the responsibility for their tasks, but also shared the pride in a job well done.

When I was moved to another department, I was replaced by a very competent engineer whose experience had given him an excellent knowledge of the men's job functions. Nevertheless, within six months the department's morale and productivity began to droop. I asked the foreman why.

"Do you know why you were able to get so much work out of those guys? Because you left them alone long enough to get the job done." The new manager, he explained, was a shirtsleeves supervisor with some very definite ideas on how to make a repair. His preconceived ideas and his inability to be open to input cut the men out of a feeling of belonging—and they, in turn, lost the desire to perform.

The Familiarity Trap.   We are often confronted with a situation that is not altogether new but, to some extent, a reproduction of a previous experience. Yet, as soon as we recognize a similarity, our search for any differences stops. The mind immediately categorizes the event and emits a reaction that has been accepted as correct based on previous experience. And that is where the "familiarity trap" begins.

Where does it end? When a manager judges an employee hastily based on his or her knowledge of a past employee, it ends with a personnel problem; when a manager who's "done it all" decides that he knows better than his highly skilled subordinates, it can end with a communication problem; and when a supervisor makes unilateral decisions based on her "experience," without asking for employee input, it can end with a departmental crisis.

"I've Heard It All Before."   The manager who makes this claim had better be right; chances are, he won't be hearing much in the way of input from his employees. The instant he closed his mind, he also closed the doors to communication.

Keeping an Open Mind.   Minds are like parachutes; they only function when open. Although a closed mind is often the result of our insecurities, most managers find that taking even the first small step toward establishing a free-flowing dialogue with subordinates piques their curiosity—the more they know, the more they want to know.

These guidelines can be your first step toward breaking the barrier of preconceived ideas. See if your employees don't meet your communication effort halfway.

What's New? To the manager who has tapped into the flow of information available at his or her office, everything! When effective listening starts, creativity flourishes: new ideas, new solutions, new perspectives abound.

If you've recently been promoted or recruited, focus on the *differences* between your new position and your previous job to start clearing away those preconceived ideas. If you're more of a departmental fixture, refresh your perspective by devoting a day to awareness. How have your duties expanded—or retracted—since a year ago? What changes have your employees noticed? *Ask them*—their answers will not only reaffirm your feeling of "newness," but will kick off a process that brings constant renewal—the listening process.

It's Not What You Know, It's Who You Know. Who do *you* know who can tell you how to operate every piece of equipment in your department from the Xerox machine to the bottle capper?

Put aside your preconceived notions about your own limitless expertise and get to know those individuals who know every facet of your department best—your employees. The sweetest sounds to your subordinates' ears are open-ended questions that let them know they are respected and needed. Take the time to ask your in-house panel of experts how *they* think your team could improve production or solve a problem, and really *listen* to their answers. Open your mind and you unlock your depart-

MINDS ARE LIKE PARACHUTES:
THEY ONLY FUNCTION
WHEN OPEN.

IT'S NOT WHAT YOU KNOW,
IT'S WHO YOU KNOW.
GET TO KNOW THOSE
INDIVIDUALS WHO KNOW
EVERY FACET OF YOUR
DEPARTMENT BEST—
YOUR EMPLOYEES.

ment's potential. Stop listening and you stop learning. Stop listening and soliciting input and you forfeit the right to hold your people accountable for their performance.

TALKING TOO MUCH, TOO OFTEN: LISTENING TO OUR OWN NEEDS

The plain truth is that you cannot listen while you are talking. We are each blessed with two ears and one mouth. The wise manager will use that physiological fact as a constant reminder of the most effective listening/speaking ratio.

Understanding Why We Talk.   The reason why you, as a manager, may be talking too much today is the same reason you uttered your very first words: You are cajoled to talk, compelled to talk, invited to talk, even begged to talk because what you say has the power to make yourself—and others—feel good.

"I'm Here."   Every sentence you speak, no matter what its content or message, announces your presence. Utter the simplest phrase and you pat yourself on the back for being alive; deliver a monologue on your latest achievements and you've established—at least for yourself—your status among the world's "haves."

In some circles where social climbing is not an occasionally played indoor sport but a necessity, the quality of one's words is taken as an indication of the quality of one's life, education, and mind.

Our human compulsion to speak fulfills our need to inform the world that we have arrived, we are arriving, or that we expect to arrive sometime in the near future.

As I Was Saying.   The need to talk *at* and not *to* other people can be traced to nervousness, insecurity, and

WE ARE EACH BLESSED WITH
TWO EARS AND ONE MOUTH—
A CONSTANT REMINDER
THAT WE SHOULD LISTEN
TWICE AS MUCH AS WE TALK.

WHEN WE TALK AT AND NOT TO
OTHER PEOPLE, IT IS AS IF WE
ARE TALKING TO OURSELVES.

sometimes guilt. Any apprehensions the speaker may have about her image in the listener's eyes compels her to keep her emotional distance. The speaker's communication becomes more and more one-sided until she is, in effect, talking to herself.

Learning to Speak the Native Tongue.   I was twenty-two and fresh out of college when I got my first job as a production foreman in a linen mill. Needless to say, I was eager to put my skills to work for me and to prove myself as a manager. Unfortunately, I was so eager that I began to talk *at* and not *to* my new staff, made up entirely of middle-aged women.

As is the case in many offices and factories, seniority meant clout in my sewing room, so when my first set of directives was prepared, I made sure I presented them to the woman who had been there long enough to make an imposing impression on her peers—a woman known as Big Helen.

She greeted me as soon as I approached her. "Hello, Kevin," she said. I was pleased—here was a woman who seemed genuinely to welcome my input despite the thirty-year gap in our ages! Encouraged, I began to outline my decisions about the way the sewing room had to be run. "Okay, Kevin!" she answered, and hurried back to her station, I *thought*, to put my insights into operation. Yet, by that afternoon, it was business as usual—and I decided to speak to Big Helen again.

I never asked Helen for her input. I never asked whether she had any questions that might have prevented her from implementing my suggestions. Instead, I reiterated my plans for reorganizing the sewing room. "Okay, Kevin!" said Big Helen, who turned on her heel and headed straight back to her station.

Shortly thereafter, I saw Helen in conversation with her coworkers, which I took as a good sign. Yet, by the next morning the sewing room was going full force, and none of my suggestions had been taken. By noon I had sought the advice of the previous production foreman.

"I think I'm having a little personnel problem," I began. However, as I outlined my confrontation with Big Helen, his smile became harder to suppress.

"Well, what did you want Helen to do, Kevin?" he asked. I briefed him on my plan.

"Then we'd better go tell her in Polish because the only words of English she knows are 'Hello, Kevin' and 'Okay, Kevin.'"

No doubt about it, my nerves and eagerness had gotten the better of me. But although my managerial "deafness" was pointed up by my inability to perceive even the most basic data about my employees, talking too much too often has the same effect in *any* language.

The Listener as Stationary Target.   When a speaker talks without listening, to himself or to others, he is communicating directly from his ego. As a part of his image-building system, he is apt to target his audience by telling them what he thinks they want to hear. Immediately gratified, and suddenly *very* interested in this one-way conversation, the listener is then encouraged to do the same. This kind of superficially satisfying exchange can go on indefinitely, often with devastating results.

Bill, the manager of the advertising sales department of a large radio station, prided himself on his persuasive skills. His uncanny ability to target and sell potential advertisers on the advantages of buying air time had taken him all the way from sales assistant to department manager in three short years.

But now Bill was in jeopardy; after two months, the department record was less than a standout. To assuage his ego, Bill "covered" for his people—and himself—with higher-ups, reporting that revenues were never higher. It wasn't a lie, really; Bill was convinced that his managerial skills would ultimately bring the department around. And that was why, with complete assurance, he announced the department's success to his staff—and raised their sales quotas by twenty-five percent.

Bill's subordinates were confused. They knew that business was far from booming; yet, their manager had made them examples to the entire organization. He had told them what they wanted to hear—the least they could do was return the favor.

For a while, Bill's employees really tried to pick up their flagging sales ratios, but when that didn't work, there was only one alternative—they began to assure Bill of their successes. When the sales figures were tabulated at the month's end, the department's rate had plummeted. Bill's people were taken off the hook and Bill was put on probation.

If Bill had opened the lines of honest communication, his employees could have offered him solutions to their sales problems; but a manager who listens to his ego and neglects to be honest with himself forces his subordinates to limit their responses.

Are You Talking Too Much?
A Manager's Quiz

Answer yes or no:

1. Are any of these expressions a part of your repertoire?

> Are you listening to me?
> Did you hear what I said?
> Now listen to what I'm going to tell you.
> You really need to hear this.
> Listen up.
> Now pay attention.

2. Do your clients, customers, and subordinates often ask you to repeat statements or instructions?

3. Do you find yourself interrupting others, or are you tempted to interrupt others with your thoughts or ideas?

4. When communicating with slow, deliberate speakers, do you find yourself finishing statements for them in the interest of saving time?

Silence: The Great Communicator.   If you answered yes to question 1 in the manager's quiz, your inability to attract and hold the attention of your clients and subordinates is showing.

Talk can be cheap—but when a manager fills the workplace with the sound of his or her own voice, talk becomes downright worthless. If you must rely upon such expressions as "Are you listening to me?" and "You really need to hear this" to differentiate your important messages from your idle chatter, you are shouting to be heard over your own "white noise."

You need to remember that silence is often the most effective way to yell at the top of your voice.

Decoding the Rapid-Fire Message.   Did you answer yes to question 2 in the manager's quiz? When others must ask you to clarify your messages, chances are you are talking too loud, too fast, *and* too often. If you feel the need to make your point quickly, you may subconsciously suspect that the listener is trying to escape you—and you may be right! The listener on the receiving end of a rapid-fire message can begin to feel like the target on a machine gun range, and nobody likes a shouter.

When you begin to feel that your listener is looking for an "out," it's time to ask a question. Invite the listener to become part of a two-way conversation; his or her interest will revive—and so will the possibilities of real communication.

Interruption: The Conversation Stopper.   If you answered affirmatively to questions 3 or 4, you are probably finishing this sentence at this very moment!

Even for the best communicators, it is sometimes difficult to allow slow and deliberate speakers to complete

FINISHING STATEMENTS FOR OTHERS WILL DIMINISH THEIR DESIRE TO COMMUNICATE.

their statements. Our humanitarian instinct compels us to help them out, to capsulize what we are *sure* they mean to say, to eliminate those awkward conversational pauses. Yet, interruption not only deters your ability to listen, it destroys a speaker's desire to communicate with you, frustrates the speaker, and sets up a competition for center stage that *cannot* be won.

The Interruption Game: The Managerial Power Play. It is a manager's responsibility to control and direct the energies of a department; yet, when your desire to control makes your subordinates feel like departmental pawns, you are playing a game that destroys morale, undermines team spirit, and stops communication cold. In short, *you lose.*

"I Know As Much As You Do—and More": The Final Move. Overheard in a textile factory: "Good news, boss," said the foreman.

"I know just what you were going to say," responded the manager. "Production is up 20 percent."

"Oh, so you know? Well—sorry I bothered you."

The manager may have won this little battle for one-upmanship, but he's lost the war. The foreman isn't likely to sacrifice his feeling for accomplishment to the manager's ego again, nor is he likely to offer information. The manager may have succeeded in putting words into his employee's mouth, but from now on, he'll be listening to himself.

Open Mouth, Insert Foot. The more you talk, the more likely you are to make errors. What if the above conversation between the manager and the foreman had gone this way?

"Good news, boss." said the foreman.

"I know just what you were going to say," responded the manager. "Production is up 20 percent."

"Not quite—but it's *only* down by 15 percent. Oh, by the way, Mr. Johnson, your supervisor, asked me to send you along to his office when you get a chance."

THE MANAGER WHO
WINS A BATTLE FOR
ONE-UPMANSHIP COULD
EVENTUALLY LOSE THE WAR.

PATIENCE IS AN IMPORTANT
INGREDIENT FOR OPEN
COMMUNICATION.

It's only a matter of time before the manager who continues to preempt and interrupt makes a fool of him- or herself. The second guess is always the losing guess, whether it's right or wrong.

Interruption and the Apprehensive Employee. Put words in the mouth of a confident employee and you may destroy the communication process, but you leave the subordinate's ego intact; foist your thoughts on an apprehensive employee or stutterer and you reinforce the problem that prompted you to interrupt in the first place.

If you are prone to impatience when conversing with a nervous subordinate or stutterer, press your lips together—then reschedule your talk for another day. Give in to your compulsion to finish labored statements and you finish off the possibilities of communication, once and for all.

Breaking the Habit: A Manager's Guide to Interruption Intervention. Spare the employee your intrusive words or you'll spoil the communication! The following guidelines can help.

Watch Your Ps and Qs—periods and question marks, that is. Every verbal message contains *audible* punctuation; until you hear that final pause, button your lip! The wait will do you—and the communication process—good, allowing you time to absorb the message and to compose the appropriate response.

A Glass of Water—The Pause That Refreshes. If your compulsion to interrupt is stronger than your will to resist, keep your mouth occupied. Have a glass of water on hand when conversing with clients or subordinates. Sip as they speak and you will allow them time to deliver their entire message—and delay your impulse to swallow up the conversation.

Count to Three—after your communication partner has finished his or her message. The time will not only ensure that your partner has stopped talking, but it will allow you to gather your thoughts and organize your presentation.

THINKING OF RESPONSES DURING THE COMMUNICATION PROCESS: THE BIGGER FISH SYNDROME

If your communication style is to take the "conversational bait," you may be hooked by the "bigger fish syndrome," the piranha of effective listening.

An accurate response to a speaker's message is a response to his or her *total* communication. It must reflect not only the content of the message, but also the speaker's tone, the emotional tenor, and the context of the situation. But the manager who has fallen prey to the bigger fish syndrome doesn't wait long enough to absorb the entire communication; instead, he takes the first piece of conversational bait offered to him. And what he catches are bits and pieces of communication so small that they get thrown back—*at* the confused speaker.

The One That Got Away.   Periodically, I accompanied my salespeople on their calls. It gave me a chance to listen to the interaction and to observe my department's strengths and weaknesses in action.

Immediately upon entering the office of the purchasing agent for a major national company, my rep noticed a tennis trophy on the agent's credenza. The agent was only too happy to explain that it was the first trophy she had ever won and that she was especially proud to have won it during her first year after having taken up the sport.

Rather than congratulate her, my salesperson launched into a fifteen-minute monologue on the trophies *he* had won. I coughed; I cleared my throat; I watched the purchasing agent put her only trophy back on the shelf and sigh. Less than three minutes later, the meeting was over; the account lost.

How did my rep interpret the communication? He was confused. Because he stopped listening after discovering that he and the purchasing agent shared a common hobby, he felt that the call had been successful; still, he never made the sale. He was so busy telling her his "fish story" that he didn't listen when the big one got away.

That Familiar Tug.   Your need to tell your story can be a powerful urge, big enough to block your ability to listen to anything beyond the message that triggered your memory, deep enough to bury any possibility of further communication. Still, only by resisting that familiar tug can you tap into the two-way flow of communication; only by putting aside your need to be heard can you begin to really listen.

Resisting the Bigger Fish Syndrome.   Your conversational partner is just like you, with just as much—or as little—interest in your fish story as you have in his or hers. Use the following strategies to keep yourself from getting in over your head and you can tune in to what your client or subordinate is *really* fishing for.

Remember What You're There For.   When you feel the urge to regale your conversational partner with an "improved version" of the tale she's telling, *stop* and think of the reason you're together. In any directed, business communication, each speaker comes to a meeting with specific objectives or needs. What are your partner's needs? Is this story her way of wearing down your objectives or confusing the issue or merely her way of

THE BIGGER FISH SYNDROME:
THE PIRANHA
OF EFFECTIVE LISTENING.

LISTENING TO OTHERS'
STORIES CAN PROVIDE
VALUABLE INSIGHT
INTO THEIR CHARACTER.

dealing with her apprehensions? Take a moment to clarify the scenario and you'll find that your big fish story doesn't seem as big as the issue at hand.

Focus on the Theme, Not the Plot. There's a moral to every story; find the moral to your communication partner's anecdote and you'll learn more about him than what he thinks he's telling you!

Does he always cast the "other guy" as the villain? Chances are, he's reluctant to take responsibility for his deeds. If you're meeting with an employee, does he speak disparagingly of his duties? Of his peers? Tune in to his attitudes and you may get to the bottom of a departmental problem before it gets to *your* bottom line.

LACK OF INTEREST IN THE CONVERSATION: LISTENING TO YOUR PREJUDICES

This is the final stumbling block that must be overcome to open one's mind, and, in many ways, it's the most difficult.

A lack of interest in a conversation is a symptom of a larger problem: a lack of interest in the *person* with whom you are communicating. Many managers, having been selected *out* from among their lower-level peers, begin focusing their interest on their managerial colleagues from the time of their promotion. Within this peer group, communication comes easy; because they hold separate but equal positions within the company hierarchy, their views are similar, and so are their problems. And because their interests are the same, they are interested in each other. In short, they have common ground.

Yet, in terms of day-to-day departmental goals and objectives, the manager's colleagues are *not* the people who share his problems, who become partners in his decisions, and who can help him find solutions; his subordinates are.

THERE'S NOTHING IDLE ABOUT
CURIOSITY WHEN IT'S ALWAYS
ON THE JOB.

THERE IS NO GREATER
COMPLIMENT THAN
DEMONSTRATING INTEREST
IN ANOTHER HUMAN BEING.

However, because the manager has distanced himself from them, it may be difficult for him to find the common ground between him and his employees that will enable him to take a sincere interest in his people—and spark their interest in making a team effort.

The Groundless Manager. "The first of the new presses came in in July," one print supervisor at a major metropolitan newspaper told me. "Three days later, we received a memo—a *memo*—outlining a major reorganization that the manager had come up with over the weekend. When, at the end of the month, a second new press arrived, the department was 'papered' again—the manager had hired two new pressmen and duties were being reallocated. By the middle of August, we thought we were safe: To our knowledge, no new machinery was expected, and we were fully staffed. But wouldn't you know it, as soon as he'd had time to think about it, he was shifting people around again. Now nobody knows what they're supposed to be doing—and worse yet, nobody really gives a damn, either."

This manager's refusal to seek out common ground between him and his subordinates has nearly become a phobia—he is so fearful of their input that he communicates with them only on paper and invites no responses. His disinterest is obvious; he moves his men around as if they were game pieces with absolutely no thought to their preferences and their abilities. Yet, how could it be otherwise? He has distanced himself so completely from the workings of his department that he could not possibly know of his subordinates' skills and talents. His apprehensions about his own skills have made him apprehensive about communication, and now he is a "groundless" manager, the leader of a low-morale, low-productivity gripe-group, ready for a fall.

A Map to Your Department's Common Ground. Get out from behind the managerial desk, take three steps beyond your office door, and you've found it: common

GET OUT FROM BEHIND
YOUR DESK, TAKE THREE STEPS
BEYOND YOUR OFFICE DOOR,
AND YOU'VE FOUND IT:
COMMON GROUND.

ground, the key to a mutually interested, mutually dependent, totally accountable department.

From this vantage point, all you really have to do is
look around you to see the interests you share with your
subordinates: their jobs, *your* job, the department's problems, the company's strengths and weaknesses. Invite your
people to tune in to any of these subjects with you as a
group, and you can begin to tune in to their attitudes,
special skills, and personal interests. But to really motivate
those valuable employees, you must get to know them
better as individuals, and invest the time and effort to
make them want to invest *their* abilities in their jobs. The
following guidelines will get you started.

The Universal "Me." When meeting with an employee for the first time on a one-to-one basis, the silence
can be deafening. (The employee may be expecting a
reprimand rather than an open forum and might not want
to "talk" without counsel present!) Remember that, although your subordinate may not be forthcoming with
information, there is always one area of interest she cannot
resist but discuss: *herself.* A simple question like "How
long have you lived in this area, Mary?" will bring forth
some common points of interest for later discussion. Keep
transmitting your interest and you will keep the employee
at ease while encouraging her to open up. ("You mean you
moved *here*, to the land of the frozen tundra, from Los
Angeles? That must have been a shock to your system!")
Soon you will begin to know *Mary*, not just her function,
and when you do, you will begin to *learn.*

Ask Questions. Don't ask just for the sake of having
something to say, but for the sake of understanding. Make
your subordinates feel that you are interested enough in
their concerns to make them your concerns as well, and
soon they will rally to your side. Ask them how your
decisions affect them; make sure that they understand your

ASK QUESTIONS, NOT FOR
THE SAKE OF HAVING
SOMETHING TO SAY,
BUT FOR THE DESIRE
TO UNDERSTAND.

motivations. They will feel that you have their best interests at heart and can then begin to work *with* you, not against you.

Keep Your Promises.   I once had a manager who took every opportunity he could get to remind us that he had an "open-door policy." Yet, as soon as any of his subordinates approached, he was all business—too busy to stop reading, writing, and shuffling papers.

By actively expressing an interest in your employees, you have promised them your continued interest. Make eye contact, make an effort, and make time; in short, make good on your pledge and they'll make good on their commitment to you.

WHAT SHOULD YOU LISTEN FOR?
THE LITTLE THINGS—
EVERYTHING!

PART II

LEARNING TO LISTEN

THE RESPONSIBILITY FOR
A POOR DEPARTMENT
PERFORMANCE RESTS
WITH THE LEADER,
NOT THE EMPLOYEES.

3

Tuning In

"I'll Know It When I Hear It." Unfortunately, that's not necessarily true.

Katherine, the manager of a market research department of a small consumer products plant, was having a personnel (and, therefore, a morale) problem. Although she was perceptive enough to hold a casual monthly meeting with her employees to clarify goals and objectives, it seemed that her suggestions and decisions never made it out of the meeting room and into the workplace. Somehow, somewhere, they were always lost en route to their destination.

Her assistant manager, Stephen, offered his explanation of the problem. "It's human nature to cling to the familiar, to resist change," he said. "Maybe if we could offer them a bonus plan, they would be more willing to give new ideas a try."

It made sense to Katherine, and that very afternoon, she approached her manager with the plan. He turned her down.

Meanwhile, the difficulties seemed to be getting worse: Because the employees relied on out-of-date methods to get their market information, their latest project had given their marketing director a completely skewed view of

UNLESS YOU KNOW WHAT
YOU'RE LISTENING FOR,
IT MAY BE DIFFICULT
TO KNOW IT WHEN
YOU HEAR IT.

consumer needs. And the company had lost a great deal of money because of it. Again, Katherine turned to Stephen for advice.

"I think you should clean house and single out those employees who refuse to accept your decisions."

Katherine, at the end of her rope, saw no other choice and began to file the necessary papers for the dismissal of two of her subordinates. However, when approval came from Katherine's manager, it was not the employees who were let go, it was Katherine.

Interference: The Great Distorter. Katherine *was* listening, but because she was tuned in to interference—Stephen—she was acting on static, not a clear message. As soon as her assistant manager gave her conflicting messages, her antennas should have gone up; his advice did nothing for the department, but it did keep Katherine, in this case unfavorably, in her manager's eye. She allowed Stephen to undermine her authority, made her boss suspicious of her ability to lead, and, ultimately, got herself fired. Could Katherine have heard the accurate message if she had known what she was listening for? Of course. Stephen's advice always ran counter to her own instincts to listen to her employees; she should have tuned in to her own good judgment. She should have listened to the message from her boss; his refusal to her bonus plan suggestion would have told her that she was going in the wrong direction. Last, she should have *really* listened to her employees rather than threatened or cajoled; there may have been a very good reason that they could not integrate Katherine's suggestions immediately.

Unless you know what you're listening *for*, it can be difficult to know it when you hear it. It is just as important that you tune in to those pieces of information that can really make a difference to your department as to tune out those bits of useless knowledge that can become distortions.

So, what does the effective manager listen to?

LISTEN TO CONTEXT,
LISTEN FOR CONTENT,
AND YOU'LL LISTEN
EFFECTIVELY.

The Little Things—Everything!   We've all heard the expression that "little things mean a lot." This is the key to thorough listening.

Katherine, in her haste to get to the root of her departmental problem, stopped listening before she had all of the information she needed to act. If she had had the following guidelines to getting the *whole* message, she might still have her job today.

Tuning the Managerial Ear.   These three questions are most often asked by managers who realize the importance of tuning in, and the answers have been proven effective by the most successful managers in business today.

• What should I listen to? Context. Think of your working environment as the backdrop that makes your questions and problems stand out in bold relief. Listen to the particulars of that environment—your employees' productivity, the goals of your department, the objectives of the company, and even your own listening blocks—and that will begin to train your ear on your problems *and* possible solutions as well.

• What should I listen for? Content. Lend an ear to your employees' specific suggestions and comments; listen effectively to your clients' and customers' needs; then tune in to body language and written communication as well, and you hear the full range of information available to you as a manager.

• What should I try to remember? Nothing. The effective listener doesn't have to make an effort to remember the details of the information he or she hears; such a listener absorbs information like a sponge. Once you are tuned in to context and content, and you can't help but see their similarities and, perhaps most important, their differences, it is at this moment that insight begins.

Context and Content: The Verbal Agreement. When your observations of the work environment are confirmed by your employees' verbal suggestions and comments, it is "all systems go" for the effective manager. Having taken the time to listen to the background as well as the specifics, the manager has listened long enough to get the whole story and can begin to act.

Context and Content: The Communication Clash. When what you see *isn't* what you get, it's time to get down to some hard listening!

To Tom, the manager of a small field sales force, the context spoke volumes: His goals were not unattainable, yet sales were down. The situation had all the earmarks of a morale problem. Yet, before he took action, Tom questioned his reps about their productivity—and what he heard turned his perceptions around.

The efforts of his sales force were being foiled, not by a lack of motivation, but by a problem in the order-processing department, a problem that was becoming so well known that customers were placing orders with other suppliers who made conducting business easier. Tom then tuned out the symptoms and confronted the disease— solving not only his reps' problems but a burgeoning company image difficulty as well.

In our intensity to comprehend the big picture, we often ignore the very small parts that are the cornerstones of the big picture. A conflict between context and content is your cue to stop talking and start listening.

4

How to Keep Quiet and Listen

The more you talk, the less you listen—and the more you talk, the less *others* will listen.

It's not easy to keep quiet. Our minds react instantaneously to the input of others and that reaction demands an immediate outlet. Yet, when we engage our mouths the instant we engage our minds, we stop listening to others—and start listening to our own egos.

Add your two cents' worth to a conversation and that's what the communication will be worth; delay your reaction to another's thoughts and suggestions and you'll react to the *whole* message, not just the small change. These guidelines are valuable delay mechanisms that speak to the source of your desire to be heard while you listen to the speaker.

Be Pertinent.   Is your comment or anecdote pertinent to your goals or the objectives of your speaker? Let the speaker have the floor first and you'll soon discover what *he* or *she* wants to get from this conversation. Comments that are not pertinent are often perceived as *im*pertinent because they distance your communication partner from

THE MORE YOU TALK,
THE LESS YOU LISTEN,
AND THE MORE YOU TALK,
THE LESS OTHERS WILL LISTEN.

IS YOUR COMMENT PERTINENT?
IS YOUR COMMENT INFORMA-
TIVE? DO YOU HAVE YOUR
THOUGHTS IN ORDER? IF NOT,
YOU'RE BETTER OFF LISTENING.

his or her goals. Some things are better left unsaid; is your story one of them?

Be Informative. Your willingness to add *valuable* information to a conversation increases your value to your communication partner. Your insistence upon adding *extraneous* information makes you . . . well, the parallel is obvious.

Be Interested. Be honest. Dig down deep and ask yourself, "Am I talking just to make myself feel good?"

There's nothing wrong with blowing your own horn when the time is right, but if your communication partner isn't expecting it, it can be deafening. Don't let your ego monopolize the conversation.

Be Patient. Let others finish before you respond. Although your partner may have dealt some of his cards, he could be waiting to play the trump. Give him time to show his hand, or you won't be playing with a full deck.

Be Ready. Use your delay time to absorb and correlate information, and your facts and thoughts will be in order when it's your turn to speak. Your communication partner isn't there to formulate your ideas for you or to put together the bits and pieces of your thoughts. Wait for her to establish both context and content, sift for inconsistencies and conflicts, *then* offer your insights *when you're ready*. Be patient and you'll be prepared.

WE ALWAYS WONDER
WHAT A PERSON OF FEW
WORDS HAS TO SAY.

5

How to Encourage Others to Listen

As you already know, listening is a natural process that goes against human nature. As a result, the same tendencies that undermine our ability to tune in to others keep others from listening to us.

Recognize that listening is "mind over matter"—then use the following strategies to focus the minds of your listeners. (Otherwise, your message won't matter!)

1. Limit your expounding. At every business meeting or social gathering, you can see the underlying principle of this concept in action!

Tune in to any group discussion and you'll find him: the listener who just nods his head and says nothing. Now watch—notice how the speaker begins to focus eye contact and interest on him? The strength of the "silent type" is his silence—and he is applying that force directly on the speaker's insecurities.

Speak softly and carry a big message. Just as the speaker in this scenario can't resist trying to find out what's going on in the "mystery thinker's" mind, so do we all wonder what the person of few words has to say. To put this principle to work for you, limit your expounding; keep introductions and explanations clear but minimal. Concentrate your efforts on keeping the attention of your listeners and your words won't dilute the impact of your message.

The speaker who lowers voice volume increases impact. Alter your usual tone of voice—soften it, slow it down—and your listeners won't want to miss a word.

2. Make it interesting. Focus on your listeners' favorite subject—themselves. Encourage them to participate in your message ("Isn't that what you thought, Sue?") or direct your comments to each of them *by name* ("Of course, that project is Pete's baby—great job, Pete!"), and you'll foster team spirit, encourage two-way communication, *and* get their attention for as long as you need it.

3. Create the right environment. Scene: a busy, trendy, noisy restaurant in a major city. Time: any business day.

> You: "And so I thought we could get together on the venture; pool our resources, pool our people."
>
> Client, leaning forward: "*Fool* our people? For what?"
>
> You: "No—*pool* them. Cooperate."
>
> Client, cupping one hand around his ear: "Corroborate? Are you calling me a liar?"
>
> You: "What did you say is on fire?"
>
> Client: "You're right, I *am* tired. Why don't we get together some other time instead, okay?"

It is difficult enough to overcome one's own listening blocks without adding to them! When you try to make an important point under less than ideal conditions, your *message* becomes less than ideal. Make your pitch in a place where physical and mental distractions are minimal, and you'll maximize the chances that you will be heard and understood.

6

Unmasking the Fake Listener

There are two types of nonlisteners: those who let you know they are too busy or too preoccupied to listen, and the notorious "fake listener." Dealing with the first nonlistener is easy: You can reschedule your meeting for a less frenetic time or ask him to let you know when he's free. But the fake listener is *always* free—free to waste your time and let you talk until your patience, or your voice, gives out.

These guidelines will help you not only to pinpoint the fake listeners within your group, but to get their attention.

• *Fake Hallmarks.* "That's interesting." "Is that right?" "How about that?" Statements like these, which encourage you to talk while the other continues not to listen, are the hallmarks of the fake listener. When you begin to hear these meaningless replies, it's time for a challenge. "Oh, do you find that interesting? What about it in particular interests you?" The fake listener will know that you're on to him or her and will begin to listen up.

• *Body Language.* Although the fake listener may play a good verbal game, his physical prowess is usually below par. Poor eye contact, shuffling feet, busy hands, and a

THE FAKE LISTENER CAN ONLY FOOL YOU IF YOU ARE NO LISTENER AT ALL.

disinterested slump may signal that there is a slump in the communication process as well. A few pointed questions should get the ball rolling again.

• *Unrelated Response.* You are outlining your plans for an upcoming meeting and your listener responds with: "Did you hear that it's going to snow on Thursday?" You can bet that the snow job has already begun! Dig the fake listener out of his reverie by asking for his input on the direction of the meeting.

7

Listening for
Hidden Messages

What we hear isn't always the same as what's being communicated! The following phrases are used constantly in our daily business dealings, yet they are signals that the *real* communication may be lurking somewhere beneath the surface.

Read this list three times and these well-worn expressions will never sound the same to you again.

• "I know what you mean." They really don't, wish they did, and hope you'll keep talking until they do.

• "Let's be honest with each other." If you *have* been honest all along, does that mean that the speaker *hasn't*?

• "It's a special deal." If it were so special, wouldn't you have noticed?

• "Between you and me . . . ." usually ends this way: "and everyone else I tell."

• "You look great!" Did you look less than great before or has the speaker just noticed you?

WHAT WE HEAR
ISN'T ALWAYS THE
SAME AS WHAT'S
BEING COMMUNICATED.

• "We're glad you could make it." Is there some reason the speaker felt you might not come? Was he or she expressing a fear or a hope?

THE BETTER YOU LISTEN,
THE LUCKIER YOU WILL GET.

PART III

HOW TO INTERVIEW, SELECT, AND TRAIN EMPLOYEES THROUGH EFFECTIVE LISTENING

YOUR PEOPLE ARE AN
INVESTMENT—AND IN
MANAGEMENT, JUST AS
IN TAXES, IT'S NOT
WHAT YOU HAVE BUT WHAT
YOU KEEP THAT COUNTS.

THERE IS ONLY ONE PERSON
WHO CAN TELL YOU WHETHER
ANY CANDIDATE IS RIGHT FOR
THE JOB: THE CANDIDATE
HIM- OR HERSELF.

Are You an Effective Interviewer? A Manager's Quiz

Answer yes or no:

1. After an interview, do you think of questions that you *should* have asked the candidate?

2. When the interviewing process has been completed, are you still confused about the candidate's qualifications?

3. Would you feel uncomfortable in making a final decision on a job candidate solely on the basis of the interview—*without* checking references?

4. Within the past year, have you later discovered that any candidate used your job offer as a wedge to secure a higher salary from his or her employer?

5. Of the five most recently hired employees in your department, have any of them since found positions elsewhere?

Because no single aspect of managing requires greater use of one's listening skills than the selection of new employees, the above quiz is perhaps the best barometer of your ability to tune in to the strengths, weaknesses, and needs of the people you hire. For every no you answered, you deserve a bonus—your listening skills have saved you both time and money. But for each yes you answered, you, your company, and your employees have paid dearly—in dollars and morale.

Research studies indicate that the cost of hiring a new employee now exceeds $1,000. Add to that the high-priced time of the managerial interviewer, the cost of training (estimated at an additional $2,000 to $4,000), and time wasted on interoffice disruption, and it becomes obvious that doing a poor job in selecting an employee impacts directly on the departmental budget—and on your ability to manage effectively.

Managers who feel they are working too hard in selecting and training new employees may not be listening hard enough. But active, aggressive listening from the time of the first communication (the résumé) between a prospective employee and a firm, through the last opportunity a manager has to objectively assess an individual's capacity to perform a job (the interview) will save the manager time and effort while ensuring a smooth transitional period for the entire department.

In Part III you utilize all the skills you learned in Part II of this book to:

Tune in to the résumé to eliminate time-consuming meetings with unsuitable candidates;

Listen during the interview to determine whether the candidate will fit into the company before a commitment has been made to that individual; and

Follow through to the training period to accelerate learning, smooth assimilation, and prevent costly employee "fallout."

Remember, your people are an investment. And in management just as in taxes, it's not what you have but what you keep that counts.

8

The Résumé of Robert Smith

To emphasize the points of listening during the interview process, the following scenario is presented. You are the senior engineering manager of a heavy industrial equipment manufacturer, and your company has an opening for a tool crib supervisor. The job requires supervisory skills and technical knowledge of machine parts. You have received the following résumé from Robert Smith in response to your ad in a trade magazine.

RÉSUMÉ

Robert Smith
999 Johnson Street
Chicago, IL 60104
312-555-1000

EDUCATION:
Graduate of Chicago High School, 1960—Drafting
Major
Attended various management seminars AMA

EXPERIENCE:
Jackson Company, March 1980–Present
Machine Parts Manager
Responsible for control of all tools and parts
distributed to maintenance and engineering
group. Supervise tool crib attendants and inven-
tory control clerk.
*G & L Engineering, January 1961–December
1980*
Engineering Draftsman
Responsible for design and updating of machine
and equipment drawings of customers. Received
draftsperson of the year award in 1973 and 1977.
Company acquired by C&B Engineering in 1980;
drafting departments consolidated and moved to
Dallas, TX.
Personal: Married, three children
Hobbies: Bowling, hunting, and reading
References: Furnished upon request

Having read the résumé carefully, tuning in to what Bob Smith says as well as what he does not say, you begin to focus on how closely the candidate's needs mesh with your own.

What Bob Smith's résumé says:
1. The candidate is interested in the job you offer.
2. The candidate has a technical knowledge of machine parts.
3. Bob Smith has some supervisory experience.
4. The candidate has risen to a supervisory position from the design end of the business.

What Bob Smith's résumé does not say:
1. Why the candidate is seeking a new job.
2. How long he has held a supervisory position.
3. What is the extent of his technical knowledge.
4. Whether he has the right chemistry to fit into your organization.

On the basis of Bob's experience, track record, and interest, you schedule an interview for the following morning.

IF YOU, AS THE INTERVIEWER, FIND YOURSELF TALKING MORE THAN 20 PERCENT OF THE TIME, THERE IS A GOOD CHANCE YOU WILL NEVER HEAR THE INFORMATION NECESSARY TO MAKE AN OBJECTIVE DECISION ON THE CANDIDATE.

9

The Interview: An Exercise in Effective Questioning and Listening

During any interview, there is only one person in the room who can give you the information you will need to decide whether a candidate is well suited for the job—the candidate. Therefore, your goal during this crucial first meeting is to allow candidate Bob Smith the freedom to speak while enhancing your ability to really *hear* the information that only he can offer. In other words, the interview is Bob's chance to talk, talk, talk—and your golden opportunity to listen and *learn*.

There are only three reasons for you, as the interviewer, to be talking while you are evaluating Bob for the job:

1. To put him at ease and briefly describe the job opening.

2. To ask pertinent questions.

3. To sell Bob on the job if you feel there is competition for his talents.

If you, as the interviewer, find yourself talking more than twenty percent of the time, there is a good chance that you will not secure the necessary information to make an objective decision on the candidate.

PUTTING THE CANDIDATE AT EASE

Why is Bob apprehensive? Besides the usual nervousness that most people feel when put "under a spotlight," Bob is apprehensive because there is one thing standing between him and the kind of career move he wishes to make—*you*.

A candidate can be sure of only one result as he or she enters an interview: either a bridge toward his or her goals or an insurmountable barrier. As an interviewer, if you use the first few minutes of the interview to reassure Bob that you respect him as a person and as a professional, he will come to view you as a partner in his future. As a result, Bob will relax, drop his guard, and allow the communication to flow freely.

Begin by asking general questions about Bob's hobbies or other more personal bits of information included on his résumé. Let Bob know that you are interested in him as a person, and you have established a line of communication that is as nonthreatening as it is revealing.

Offer Bob a brief history of the company and job opening, and you'll let Bob know that you are seriously considering him as a potential employee. Keep this introductory material short, however; a lengthy or in-depth explanation may flood the candidate's mind with questions and limit his ability to communicate openly.

Create the right environment and you'll reassure Bob

that you value his time. Never accept phone calls, allow interruptions, or stop to take notes! These divergences convince a prospective employee of your disinterest and may cause you and the candidate to lose your continuity of thought.

Finally, get out from behind your desk. There is no office accoutrement that communicates as clearly or as loudly as the "managerial desk." Physically, it is nearly a wall between you and the candidate. Symbolically, it is a constant reminder of the distance between your ranks.

Whenever possible, seat yourselves facing each other, on neutral ground. Make Bob comfortable and you'll encourage a more even type of communication throughout the interview process.

ASKING THE RIGHT QUESTIONS

• What do you consider your strengths and your weaknesses?

• Where do you envision yourself ten years up the road?

• Why do you feel that you're the most qualified for this position?

How often have you heard these questions . . . or used them yourself? Was your response, "Here we go again . . ."? These questions have been overused, abused by interviewers who may either be inexperienced or unable to improvise more personalized questions—questions for which the interviewee may not have a prepared answer.

Each time you ask any of these questions of a potential employee, you lose a chance to learn something truly valuable about that candidate. Each time you interview

GOLD IS ONLY
FOUND BY SIFTING
THROUGH ROCK AND SAND.

EFFECTIVE QUESTIONING
IS A DELICATE BALANCE
BETWEEN SECURING GOOD
INFORMATION AND
INTIMIDATING THE CANDIDATE.

without really listening, you pass up the opportunity for "effective questioning."

Effective questioning *is*:

• Maintaining the delicate balance between securing good information and not intimidating the candidate.

• The art of keeping questions open-ended and objective during the initial fact-finding portion of the interview. ("How has the economy affected the Jackson Company, Bob?")

• The key to successfully evaluating a candidate's technical and supervisory skills while encouraging him to speak freely. ("Bob, we are thinking of changing from steel to plastic fittings on our electrical connectors. Do you have any suggestions on a supplier?")

• A positive, nonjudgmental stance that allows the candidate to reveal his character, telling you all you need to know about his ability to fit into your organization.

• A relaxed, nonthreatening method for obtaining an accurate perception of a candidate's work style. ("What aspects of your present job are the most rewarding to you, Bob?")

• A flexible strategy based upon the qualifications of the *individual* candidate rather than the qualifications of the *job*.

Effective questioning is *not*:

• Interviewing by intimidation. ("Tell me, Bob, why *weren't* you offered a job with C&B Engineering in Dallas?")

• Asking the same tired questions of each candidate.

THE ONLY WAY
TO GET THE
ACCURATE ANSWERS
IS TO ASK THE
RIGHT QUESTIONS.

THE BETTER YOU LISTEN,
THE MORE YOU LEARN
HOW LITTLE YOU KNOW.

• Asking leading, rhetorical questions. ("A great shop, isn't it?")

• Finishing statements for the candidate. ("I know just what you're going to say, Bob . . .")

Putting Effective Questioning to Work for You. Based on the job requirements and Bob's résumé, you now need to find out the following through effective questioning:

1. The true amount of supervisory experience Bob has obtained at his present job.
2. The degree of technical knowledge he possesses.
3. Why he wants to leave the Jackson Company.
4. If Bob is the right person for the job.

LISTENING FOR SUPERVISORY EXPERIENCE

Probing for technical or supervisory skills not only clarifies the depth of the candidate's knowledge, but can reveal a great deal about his character as well, if a manager remains tight-lipped. Remember that it is Bob who is under assessment today. Revealing the ins and outs of *your* professional history will only tempt him to tell you what he thinks you want to hear. Finally, keep your questions open-ended and your comments to yourself; the better you listen, the more you learn how little you know.

Is the Candidate Managerial Material? Ask Bob what part of his present job he finds most rewarding and which aspects are most frustrating. If he responds that he finds handling paperwork and dealing with details more satisfying than resolving departmental employee problems, he may have been promoted out of his area of preference.

Is Bob a Troubleshooter? One question can tell you whether Bob is ready to slip into a supervisor's shoes.

WHAT YOU DON'T KNOW
MIGHT HURT YOU;
WHAT YOU DO KNOW
WILL ONLY HELP YOU.

WHY IS EFFECTIVE
INTERVIEWING A NOBLE ART?
ASK THE RIGHT QUESTIONS
AND YOU'LL KEEP THE
CANDIDATE HONEST.

Briefly describe a common employee problem—such as a worker's chronic lateness—and ask how he would handle it. A facile answer such as "I'd fire him" indicates that Bob is hardly ready to take on a supervisory position (and may reveal that Bob may not have been altogether honest in his résumé). If, on the other hand, Bob carefully weighs factors such as the employee's past performance, length of service, and the duration of the problem, his considerations give you valuable insight into his thought processes and level of experience.

Pinpoint Bob's Experience. First follow up his response to the problem with a nonjudgmental statement to keep him off guard ("That's an interesting approach to the problem, Bob,"); then ask for the hard facts ("How long have you been a direct supervisor now?"). His answer will confirm whether he is a new supervisor, a seasoned supervisor, or merely a poor supervisor.

Unexpected confrontational questions ("Are you *sure* you've had supervisory experience, Bob?") will *not* startle the truth out of a candidate as some less merciful (and more aggressive) managers may believe. *Offensive questions only serve to put the prospective* employee on the *defensive*, thus ruining any chances of unguarded reply for the remainder of the interview.

LISTENING FOR TECHNICAL KNOWLEDGE

A résumé may outline the parameters of a candidate's experience, but only effective questioning can put you in touch with the specific technical and *ethical* strengths and weaknesses of each prospective employee. The following powerful strategies are guaranteed to separate the bluff from the real stuff. Use them once and you'll rely on them forever.

Loose Lips Drop Tips. If Bob feels you know very little about the technical aspects of his present job, he will *hand* you a great opportunity to assess his honesty as well as his experience. Keep your questioning objective ("How does the machine parts department at the Jackson Company manage to control inventories?") and Bob will tell you where his abilities begin—and *end*.

Never use your own background to prod answers from the candidate. Slanted questioning ("I see you came up from the design ranks as well, Bob. Is design still one of your interests?") inevitably results in slanted responses. As computer programmers say, *GIGO:* Garbage In, Garbage Out. This is the time to be vigilant about your input.

Ask for Advice.   Explain to the candidate how your present system is set up and list some of your vendors. Then set the machinery in motion by probing for specifics with questions like these:

"Bob, who do you feel makes the best drill bits?"

"Bob, we are thinking of changing from solvent cleaners to water-based products. Do you have any suggestions on a vendor?"

Now you can just sit back and nod your head, even if you feel that he's snowing you.

Playing Your Hand Against the Bluff.   Ready to confirm whether Bob is bluffing? Use an incorrect company name with a product to see how the candidate responds.

If the candidate answers positively to a question like "Bob, do you have the same problem of late deliveries with B&K Gears?" a warning flag should wave. If his response is rife with inconsistencies or incorrect industry terminology, you may wish to push the button on the interviewee ejection seat. But wait—at least until a nonchalant follow-up question on whom Bob normally deals with at B&K provides an uncomfortable response.

LISTENING FOR INDUSTRY KNOWLEDGE

Industry knowledge is one of the few quantitative tools a manager has with which to evaluate the candidate. While it must be understood that industry knowledge is always commensurate with experience (thus excusing, to some extent, low-level employees who are looking to make a step up), this body of information is an unfailingly accurate barometer of both a candidate's depth of knowledge and interest in his or her job.

Getting Down to Details.   When I interviewed to fill sales positions, I always asked the names of people whom candidates had actually called on at specific companies. The manner in which they answered this question let me know whether they were calling on the decision maker or whether they were truly calling on the account at all. More than half the time this was an eliminating question for the candidate.

Interviewing to fill a nonsales slot? Tune in to recent mergers, acquisitions, takeovers, and other bits of industry information, and you'll soon learn whether this candidate deserves tuning out.

LISTENING FOR CREDIBILITY

The time to find out whether the candidate is a straight shooter is during the interview, not after he or she is hired. Give candidates enough leeway to show their true colors and encourage them to talk. Remember, keep the door of communication open and, one way or another, the candidate will walk through it.

KEEP THE DOOR OF
COMMUNICATION OPEN AND,
ONE WAY OR THE OTHER,
THE CANDIDATE IS SURE
TO WALK THROUGH IT.

WHAT ARE A CANDIDATE'S MOST
DANGEROUS QUALIFICATIONS?
APPROXIMATELY . . .,
ABOUT . . ., AND I'D
ESTIMATE. . . .

Playing the Dunce. When I receive comments like "I'm not sure who is the key decision maker now that the company has changed hands," I never respond with a challenge (or the right answer!) but with a nonjudgmental comment—"I know just what you mean. That's a real problem in the industry." The candidate is relieved, remains open, and, in most cases, will continue to talk him- or herself right out of a job.

Clarifying the Candidate's Answer. Effective listening means actively, aggressively pursuing that which you need to hear.

Every candidate, whether due to genuine anxiety or a desire to avoid touchy subjects, will at one time or another gloss over an answer that otherwise might have given you insight into his or her credibility. When a response strikes you as practiced or ambiguous ("The move to Dallas was a boon to G&L Engineering, but it would not have been beneficial to me."), it is time to separate fact from innuendo.

To get at the truth of the matter, restate specific points that the candidate seems to want to gloss over. A nonthreatening nudge toward clarification, such as "Bob, what you are saying is that you were actually offered a job to move to Dallas but turned it down because you wanted to stay in Chicago," will force the candidate to either answer "Yes, that is correct," or begin hedging: "Well, they didn't actually offer me a job, but they knew I would not relocate if they extended an offer."

Clarifying the Candidate's Most Dangerous Qualifications. "Approximately . . .," "I'd say *about* . . .," "I'd estimate . . ."—these disclaimers are without a doubt the most dangerous qualifications any candidate can bring to an interview. Restate *any* response that contains these modifiers as soon as you hear them. "So, Bob, you say you've been supervising for *about* two years. Am I correct in assuming that that means you've been in charge for two full years?" Your question will either highlight the truth ("It was two years last month.") or the exaggeration ("Well, it's really been about a year and a half, but who's counting?").

Remember, listening is the accurate perception of what is being communicated. If you have any doubt regarding an important issue, a restatement of your perception will press the point—and pressure the candidate either to validate your position or lose your trust.

LISTENING TO DETERMINE WHY THE CANDIDATE IS IN THE JOB MARKET

At this point, Bob may seem like a manager's dream come true: He knows his stuff, seems scrupulously honest, and, best of all, is sitting within arm's reach. But before you start to woo him with dental plans and expense accounts, *stop*. Every mis-hire puts a dent in your departmental budget. If Bob is planning to use you as a wedge against his present employers or a hedge against unemployment, making an offer means making a costly mistake. Use effective questioning to get to the bottom of Bob's motivations before he gets to your bottom line.

Is Bob Still Working?   More than twenty-five percent of all résumés I receive give the impression that the candidate is still employed, when, in truth, he or she is out of a job.

Whether or not Bob has time on his hands is easily identified by his flexibility in scheduling the interview. If you find that Bob can come at any time, it is not out of line to ask him if the date and time will interfere with his work schedule. Most candidates will explain their present situation when asked.

If you feel that the prospective employee is hedging, follow up with a direct question: "Bob, are you still working for the Jackson Company in the capacity of machine parts manager?" If he is not straightforward about his status, keep the appointment to hear him out, but remember—a candidate who is not working but refuses to discuss the situation may be a problem. Take a chance on him and you take a chance with your own internal credibility.

Why Is Bob Unhappy? Following are two possibilities you should pursue.

1. I love my job; it's the work I hate. If any hint of dissatisfaction surfaces in Bob's discussion of his job functions, tune in *immediately*. Bob may tell you that if his hands were not tied (and if his manager would have only listened), he could have installed a new system for controlling chemical waste that would have saved the company thousands of dollars. Encourage Bob to detail his plan— chances are, he'll be happy to point up his own brilliance. Meanwhile, Bob has given you all the information you need to determine whether he is a "thinker, not a doer," whether his suggestions make sound business sense or if his unhappiness is unjustified.

2. The Boss: The Workman's Burden. Since a common source of discontent is conflict with a supervisor, the interviewer should probe for those specific factors and personality traits that Bob finds disconcerting in his present manager. Do you have similar traits? Since Bob has a rather stable employment record, are his criticisms due to a recent change in bosses or other recent innovations? If so, ask him how his new boss differs from his old manager. Bob's answer will project his image of the kind of system in which he works well. If Bob chafes under tight controls, and that happens to be your style of management, the chemistry between you and Bob may be explosive.

Dissatisfaction Guaranteed. If the candidate has an unstable employment history and has changed jobs often

MOST OF US KNOW
HOW TO KEEP SILENT,
BUT FEW OF
US KNOW WHEN.

WHEN THE CANDIDATE
MENTIONS MONEY FIRST,
CHANCES ARE THE
INTERVIEW POTENTIAL
IS BANKRUPT.

(every two to three years), it is important to determine whether he is a victim of circumstance or a victim of his own ego. A litany of complaints about companies you know to be viable employers will signal that your candidate is chronically dissatisfied—and that he is apt to grow dissatisfied with your company as well.

If, on the other hand, the candidate has been outplaced due to consolidation, a change in management, or company relocation, carry on with your assessment, but be sure to have him evaluated by a number of other managers before a decision is made on employment.

Is Bob Using You as a Lever? Whenever a candidate pursues the economic issues before analyzing the job functions, there is a good chance that he or she is looking to use you as a lever for advancement in his or her present job.

When Money Talks, the Candidate Walks. I once interviewed a bright, creative candidate whose major concern was bargaining for $1,000 in additional salary. After some negotiation, I agreed to the sum. Shortly thereafter, the candidate accepted the position and passed the company physical. But on the day he was to start, where was my bright, new prospect? Back at his old company with a $3,000 raise in pay. If I knew then what I know now, I would have *listened* to him *tell me* that he was using me as a wedge to get a higher salary from his employer. But, after that course in the school of hard knocks, I never counted on anyone on board until he or she walked through the door. And I *never* negotiated for small amounts of money once a salary, with an acceptable range, was offered to an individual.

Money should not be a factor until both you and the candidate decide there is a good mutual fit. If Bob asks about remuneration and is not, by industry standards, grossly underpaid, you should be on your guard. When the

TO SELL THE RIGHT
INDIVIDUAL ON THE
JOB, FOCUS ON THE
CANDIDATE'S NEEDS,
NOT YOURS.

candidate mentions money first, chances are the interview potential is bankrupt.

Are Opportunities Limited for Bob? The best candidates aren't waiting for opportunity to knock down the door and come in. The best candidates already have one foot through the door.

If Bob is not dissatisfied with his responsibilities but feels that opportunities are limited due to his lack of seniority or the absence of company growth, he may be the employee you are looking for. Ask Bob if he feels that his present company's objectives measure up to his own. He may tell you that his present employer, a company con cerned with just getting through the fiscal year, is inviting a buy-out, a stance that puts Bob's plans on the line. He may also voice dissatisfaction with his present work arrangements or salary and is looking for a job that will carry him through retirement.

If, during this stage of the evaluation, you are convinced that Bob clearly wants to invest his time and effort in a company that will become a partner in his future, you can begin to determine Bob's salary requirements—and start to sell him on the idea of making a move to your company.

SELLING THE CANDIDATE ON THE JOB

By now you are familiar with Bob's strengths and weaknesses, his reasons for wanting to leave his present position, and his apprehensions about the change. In effect, Bob himself has told you how most effectively to sell him on the job you offer! Now make your presentation—and utilize the following guidelines to keep the focus on *Bob's* needs, not yours:

• Use the comments that the candidate has offered throughout the interview to reaffirm the benefits of the position you offer, while not degrading his present position. ("Not only would I like to make use of your supervisory skills, Bob, I'd like to expand them.")

• Let the candidate know that he has the qualifications you are looking for and that you are interested in extending an offer. ("How soon could you make the move, Bob?")

• Remove any apprehensions Bob has concerning the job, company, or financial factors. ("The position we hope you'll fill, Bob, is an expansion position.")

• Make sure Bob doesn't leave with any unanswered questions. Once Bob leaves your office, your ability to influence his decision diminishes.

• Never stretch the truth! You have already ascertained the extent of Bob's industry knowledge. Expect him to cull his reliable sources for information. And if he discovers any differences between your presentation and company policy, expect him to take his job search elsewhere.

GUIDELINES FOR AN AMICABLE DISMISSAL

• Don't lead a candidate on. If Bob isn't right for the job, dismiss him professionally. His time is as valuable as yours.

• Let the candidate arrive at the decision that this job is not for him. Your duty is to release the candidate back into the community with a positive feeling about himself—

and about your company. Cordial parting comments like "I really enjoyed this meeting, but I don't feel we can offer you more than your present position" will allow the candidate to feel that the decision was mutual.

• Give the candidate at least *one* objective reason for your decision. I always took the time to explain briefly how my needs and the candidate's objectives failed to mesh. The prospective employee can learn what you are looking for only if you let him know. You'll help today's dismissal become tomorrow's best bet.

• Remember, it's a small world, particularly in closely knit industries. Take a moment to make the departing candidate as comfortable as possible. After all, who knows—maybe someday that candidate will be interviewing *you*.

Summary:
A Manager's Guide to Effective Questioning

Review this brief guide to effective questioning to keep the focus of your interview *off* of you and *on* the candidate.

When interviewing, ALWAYS:

1. Keep the candidate relaxed.

2. Ask comfortable, general questions at the beginning of the communication. "Do you have a few minutes to talk about your experiences at the Jackson Company?" "Tell me about your hobbies."

3. Let the candidate talk. Be patient. A pause may be needed to allow the candidate to gather his or her thoughts.

4. Develop a short list of questions as a guide to securing the appropriate information.

WHEN DISMISSING A
CANDIDATE, REMEMBER:
TODAY'S UNSUITABLE
CANDIDATE MAY BE
TOMORROW'S BEST BET.

INTERRUPTING OR FINISHING
STATEMENTS FOR THE
CANDIDATE IS LIKE
TALKING TO YOURSELF:
YOU FEEL GOOD
BUT LEARN NOTHING.

NEVER:

1. Ask leading rhetorical questions that will force a biased response. "You believe in the merits of rising up from the ranks, don't you?"

2. Interrupt the candidate.

3. Finish statements by anticipating what is going to be said by the candidate. If a manager continues to interrupt, the candidate will become frustrated and withdraw.

THE DANGER OF SINK-OR-SWIM
TRAINING IS THAT IT IS
TRAINING—IT IS TRAINING
FOR FAILURE.

10

Effective Orientation Means Effective Listening

"To get the job, I first had to submit two original ads," one advertising copywriter said. "They were, in effect, a qualifying round because it wasn't until a week later that the copy chief set up the first interview. That was followed by a second interview, which included the agency founder and the creative director. The third interview, nearly a month after my initial contact with the agency, was my chance to meet the rest of the department. I remember thinking, 'Finally, an agency that really cares enough to stop the advertising revolving door.'

"Then came my first day of work. The copy chief who spent so much time on the interview showed me into an office, handed me a box of supplies, and said, 'Oh, by the way—there's a creative meeting tomorrow at nine.' It was clearly sink or swim—so I started swimming."

A Blueprint for Failure.   The danger of sink-or-swim training is that it *is* training: It is a training for failure. In

PREVIOUS EXPERIENCE
IS NOT AN EQUITABLE
SUBSTITUTE
FOR ORIENTATION
AND TRAINING.

time, even the best new hires will ultimately sink—and what will pull them under is not the weight of what they didn't learn, but the burden of what they *did* learn.

Lessons from the School of Hard Knocks. Just three months of SOS orientation teaches your new employees the following lessons:

• Not to ask questions: a practice that encourages error.

• To rely on what they know: a survival technique that temporarily rewards a new employee for bringing old, possibly unsuccessful work habits into a new situation.

• To get by: to cultivate those skills that superficially "cover" confusion or ignorance.

• That the manager is inaccessible and cannot be considered a source of information on any level.

• That the only value of this job is its future value—as a jumping-off point to a more fulfilling, less confusing position.

Listening for a Smooth Transition. Any manager who is really tuned in to the needs of his or her employees understands this axiom of effective listening: A smooth transition is never a *quiet* transition. Assimilation means change, and change means adjustment, insecurity, and even confusion, not just for the newly hired employee, but for the entire department.

Nothing can shake morale or bring productivity to a screeching halt like a slow, unsteady, mismanaged orientation period. Leave a hesitant, new employee—no matter how experienced—to sink or swim, and you can expect the

A SMOOTH TRANSITION IS NEVER A QUIET TRANSITION.

newcomer's insecurity to spread throughout the department. The newly hired employee spends more time wondering what he or she should be doing than taking action. Soon the rest of the staff begins to resent accommodating this dead weight—and to doubt your hiring judgment. A manager who turns a deaf ear at this crucial time invites interpersonal problems, a decline in morale, and a total cessation of work processes.

Training Your Ear on the Orientation Period.   Managers have told me that the following guidelines for smoothing the transitional period have cut assimilation time in their departments *by half.* No matter how tightly you run your ship, remember this: Support your staff and they will support you. Set aside just a few minutes each day to tune in to their needs and the needs of a new employee, and the next thing you'll hear is "full speed ahead."

• Prepare your staff for the arrival of a new employee *before* he or she comes on board. Clarify the new arrival's duties and parameters of authority. If the department is expanding, explain any reorganization of responsibilities that may affect your employees. Above all, don't use the new hire to spark competition within the department or as a vague threat.

• Take the time to introduce the new employee to his or her peers, and while introductions are made, be sure to explain each coworker's function. If work is commonly passed along from worker to worker in a progression, introduce the employee to each colleague in the order that his or her assignments will be passed. This gives the new hire a mental map of the departmental terrain.

• If protocol permits, follow up the introductions with a departmental lunch or casual gathering. This not only

CORRECT—OR PRAISE—
THE NEW EMPLOYEE
IMMEDIATELY AND OFTEN.
WITHHOLDING EITHER
IS WITHHOLDING TRAINING.

fosters a feeling of camaraderie, but it opens the door for communication between the employees and the manager.

• Ask the new employee how various departmental functions were handled or monitored in his or her past place of employment. Then use the differences or similarities as a comparison point for clarifying the inner workings of your department. Making the new environment seem less alien will help the employee to integrate faster.

• Listen for hesitancy—it is a sign that the employee is confused or unsure of company procedure. When you ask a new employee to carry out a task and his or her response is not immediate, chances are that you have not given the information needed to carry out the job. Clarify both the task and the procedure until the employee seems confident.

• See to it that the new hire has a good source of information in the department other than you. A new employee, who is usually very conscious that he or she is being evaluated, may feel more secure asking a peer for help with minor matters.

• Correct—or praise—immediately and often. Waiting or withholding correction or praise is equally damaging.

• Most of all, *be available*. Drop in to check on the new employee at least twice a day to answer questions, probe for problems, and just to establish a bond. And be certain to keep your door open to seasoned department staffers as well; they can clue you in to disrupted work patterns or areas of confusion that you may have overlooked.

THE MANAGER'S CREED

1. My first responsibility is to my people and to the families that will be touched directly or indirectly by my words or actions.

2. My second responsibility is to my company. I will strive to ensure that my tasks and the tasks of my subordinates are performed to quality standards consistent with the company's philosophy.

3. My third responsibility is a commitment to growth. My staff is a valuable company resource. Their input will enable the company to forge ahead without sacrificing the quality that is a part of the company charter. I will welcome and encourage their ideas without taking them as my own.

4. My fourth responsibility is to myself. My decisions affect not only the company, but the social and economic well-being of my staff. My good judgment, not my personal ego, will be my guide.

PART IV

MANAGING THROUGH EFFECTIVE LISTENING

THE MANAGER'S AUTHORITY
DOES NOT STOP AT THE OFFICE
DOOR, BUT AT THE EMPLOYEE'S
KITCHEN TABLE.

11

Realizations about
a Manager

There are two simple facts you may not know—or may be afraid to face—about your job: The first is the bare-bones truth about what your employees *really* bring home with their briefcases every night; the second is an ego-blasting bit of knowledge that ineffective managers never face. Together they are the bottom-line basics of management, the plain facts that can make the difference between success and failure.

1. The manager is one of the most important people in the subordinate's life.
2. Most subordinates know more about the intricacies of their jobs than even the best manager.

THE MANAGER'S IMPORTANCE

When you are the sole decision maker who wields the power to promote, hire, and fire, to bestow raises and to deny them, your influence on the lives of your subordinates does not stop at the office door. Indeed, the extent of your authority reaches all the way to the one place most symbolic of your power to provide and take away—the employee's kitchen table.

As a child, I was amazed at the amount of time my family spent watching the dinner grow cold as my mother interpreted and reinterpreted a single off-the-cuff statement made to her by her boss during the day. It didn't take long before the entire family came to resent the managers and the company for detracting from the time our mother spent with us—and for ruining our meals.

The Bomb in the Briefcase.   No matter how circuitous its route, trouble *always* returns to its place of origin—and when an on-the-job problem makes the commute from the workplace to the employee's home, then back to the office, it can pack a positively explosive punch.

For the manager of the distribution department of a major paper manufacturer, it had been a bad week. Business was booming, but he had lost two of his most valued employees, one to an early retirement and one to a more lucrative position. He was operating with a skeleton crew and under enormous pressure.

Therefore, on Friday when his inventory clerk asked for his two weeks vacation, the manager had no choice but to say no. And because the denial was never explained, the clerk had no choice but to argue his case before a more responsive jury—his disappointed family.

For the next six months, the clerk kept his nose to the grindstone, convincing the manager that the issue had been forgotten—until the clerk tendered his resignation. The new job offered him more money and more responsibility, he explained; yet, when the manager offered to match the offer, the clerk turned him down. The clerk's family had not only encouraged him to begin his search for a new job, but had applauded his decision to accept it. His family had his best interests at heart; his manager, the clerk felt, did not.

Don't Stop Short of Your Responsibilities.   If you do, your employees will stop short of theirs. Managers' duties extend far beyond planning, organizing, budgeting, and controlling, reaching straight into the lives of their people. When you recognize that the economical and emotional well-being of your employees (and their families) are in your hands, you've taken the first step toward establishing communication. Follow these guidelines and you've opened the door:

• The families of your subordinates are neither objective nor forgetful. Take the time to resolve conflicts before they commute to the employee's kitchen table, and you'll keep work-related problems from becoming dangerous personal issues as well.

• Cultivate an interest in your employees' lives *outside the workplace*. A bond of friendship can be developed into a positive working relationship. Remain indifferent toward your employees, and they will become indifferent toward you, *and* their work.

• Never underestimate the impact of your words or actions—what may seem insignificant to you may be of paramount importance to your employees. Changing payday from Thursday to Friday, for instance, may have little effect on you, but to a factory worker who is living from hand-to-mouth, one day could seem like a lifetime, particularly if Thursday is the family's shopping day. Whenever possible, announce any policy changes in advance; give your people a chance to make the change with you.

• Don't be a paper tiger: Stop hiding behind memos! Written announcements of policy changes make valued employees feel powerless and insignificant. Gather your staff together to clarify any impending changes *verbally*, in an open forum—and encourage questions. Then

• *LISTEN!* What you'll hear is the satisfying sound of adjustment; what you'll get is a feeling of camaraderie and

STOP SHORT OF YOUR
RESPONSIBILITIES
AND YOUR EMPLOYEES
WILL STOP SHORT
OF THEIRS.

THE MANAGER IS LIKE
THE CONDUCTOR OF A
SYMPHONY: NO ONE
EXPECTS HIM TO BE
A ONE-MAN BAND.

mutual trust. Isn't that what you'd prefer your employees to take home to their families?

SUBORDINATES' KNOWLEDGE OF THEIR JOBS

Remember that most subordinates know more about the intricacies of their jobs than even the best manager. Effective managers are like symphony conductors. They are leaders who have the responsibility to see that the entire company works together to produce an ongoing harmony; and although they may not play each individual instrument with the virtuosity of a disciplined musician, they are directors who, through skill and dedication, have learned to meld the skills and dedication of the assembly to attain a melodious end result. Their jobs are based on their ability to listen.

The least effective managers, on the other hand, are the "one-man bands," those self-centered, insecure individuals who cannot delegate but insist on playing every instrument themselves. They aren't just busy blowing their own horns; they are blowing *all* the horns. It's no wonder, then, that they have little time or energy left for leadership—or listening.

MANAGERS PROMOTED FROM
WITHIN OFTEN MISS
ONE OF THE BIGGEST
CAREER OPPORTUNITIES:
THE OPPORTUNITY TO ERR.

12

Types of Managers

It is important at this point to draw a distinction between the manager who has risen from the ranks and the manager who has been recruited from the outside. Good managers are those leaders who recognize that they need the assistance of their employees just as much as their employees need their direction and guidance. Their awareness of this interdependency leads them into stable, well-formed, working relationships, which contribute to their successes and diminish the possibility of error. Although good—and bad—managers can be either recruited or promoted into their positions, the manager who rises from within the ranks faces the most difficult transition, and the biggest possibility of failure.

MANAGERS FROM THE RANK AND FILE

"He was a good worker but a bad manager." There is at least a three-to-one chance that when you hear this all-too-common evaluation, you are hearing about a manager who rose to his or her position from the rank and file.

Managers who have been promoted from within a company often bring to their new jobs a long list of preconceived notions. They know *everything*, from the

FROM RANK AND FILE TO MANAGER: AN EIGHT-POINT PLAN

1. **Be honest** with yourself and your subordinates.
2. Be willing to **admit your mistakes.**
3. Be willing to allow others to make the same mistakes you've made.
4. **Be fair.** Treat all subordinates alike, including those who had been personal friends—or adversaries.
5. **Be consistent** with discipline and praise.
6. Let your subordinates know that your success is dependent upon their performance as a team.
7. **Be patient** when you can do a job in half the time it takes a new employee.
8. **Remember where you came from:** Reprimand as you would be reprimanded; praise as you would be praised.

strengths of the top brass to the weaknesses of those employees who, only days before, were their peers, to the only "right way" to do a job. Unfortunately, what they *think* they know can prevent them from ever learning what they *need* to know. Their preconceived notions keep them from listening.

There Are Two Ways to Do Things: My Way, and the Wrong Way. To my client, an experienced businessman who operates an injection-molding operation, it seemed as though his finishing department was finished. Morale was at an all-time low; even long-term employees were opting out of the group. When the production rate had plummeted, and the scrap rate for nonrecoverable parts had risen from two to five percent, negating half of the margin in that product line, he called me in to evaluate the supervision.

The foreman of the finishing department had recently been promoted from the ranks—a reward for his well-rounded knowledge and above-average proficiency. Yet, we were not even five minutes into our initial conversation when he told me that he "was the fastest trimmer the company ever had." When he went on to say that he couldn't understand why his people could not produce at rates close to those he established when he was on the job, I knew what I had to do—and I scheduled an informal meeting with the workers for the following morning.

I opened the conversation by soliciting suggestions on how to decrease the scrap rate, but once the communication was flowing, it didn't take long before the foreman became the primary subject. I casually mentioned that I had heard that he was one of the best finishers in the company's history. "He reminds us of that every day," interjected one worker, "but this isn't the same department as the one he worked in." Within minutes, I had the whole story. The nature of the finishing operation had changed; what was a production line during the foreman's time had

LEAVING YOUR PAST
BEHIND YOU DOES
NOT MEAN FORGETTING
WHERE YOU CAME FROM.

become a custom shop where quality, not quantity, mattered. The foreman, sure that he knew what was best, berated the workers for their lack of speed rather than rewarding them for their expertise. Frustrated by their manager's negativity, the workers' self-esteem diminished—and so did the quality of their work—until the foreman opted to return to a more comfortable job in the ranks.

To Know You Is to . . . take advantage! Each day you spend in close contact with a group of peers, you contribute to their knowledge about you. As a result, by the time a rank-and-file employee accepts a promotion, her subordinates have accumulated a "book" on the new manager's attitudes, weaknesses, and approaches to accomplishing a job. The manager's challenge is twofold: She must continue to empathize with her colleagues, yet she must establish her authority as their new leader. As a "known entity," that transition is never easy—your subordinates will test you, trying both the limits of your loyalty and the parameters of your endurance.

Reassure them, through your actions, that you respect their abilities while you assert your authority by holding a brief, casual meeting on your first day in your new role. Bring up the departmental problems you discussed when you were peers and ask for suggestions. Your old "gang" will gain in self-esteem, and you will have earned their respect as an innovative, communicative leader.

Out with the Old; In with the New. These are time-honored bywords for making a smooth transition. Unfortunately, it's not always as easy as it sounds.

As an engineer, Dave was a genius. His uncanny ability to reduce any problem, no matter how complex, to its bare essentials made him the kind of troubleshooter that management was bound to notice. It wasn't long before Dave was rewarded for his expertise—and soon he became the boss.

Still, Dave never successfully made the transition from

GAINING EXPERIENCE CAN
BE COSTLY, BUT
WILL PAY BIG
DIVIDENDS IN THE
LONG RUN.

employee to manager, and the pitfall that trapped him was his brilliant past. Although Dave had been recognized for his analytical abilities, to manage efficiently he would have had to delegate those creative, analytical jobs that won him his early success. Instead, he held on to the responsibilities of his engineering position—cheating himself, and his subordinates, out of an opportunity to grow. After a short trial period, Dave returned to engineering—at another firm.

To Err Is . . . a Good Sign.   Those who never make decisions have no opportunity to err; and those who can count their mistakes on one hand can usually enumerate their experiences on the other.

It is a manager's responsibility to encourage an employee under his or her direction to experiment, especially when the innovation is the employee's own brainchild. But the manager must be prepared for error—and equipped to transform an employee's mistakes into solid learning experiences.

One of my young salespeople came to me with a problem—a new account had given her an order for $5,000 worth of product, with one stipulation: The merchandise had to be delivered overnight. In the past, this account had never expressed an interest in our company; to compound my suspicions, this rush order had been placed *regardless* of price, signaling to me that their usual suppliers might have put a stop on the company's credit. I asked the saleswoman to investigate the account, and if credit checked out, to let the order go through.

Three months later, the customer went into bankruptcy and we were out $5,000. I asked the saleswoman if she had investigated the account, as I had suggested. She had not. After some fidgeting, she asked me if I was going to put her on suspension. I responded that I would not. She asked if I planned to fire her. "Hell, no," I answered. "I just spent $5,000 training you!" The saleswoman went on to become a regional manager, and, to the best of my

WHEN IGNORANCE GOES
INTO ACTION,
LEARNING STOPS.

knowledge, she never fails to ask her young salespeople to verify a new account's motivations.

If the amount of the order had been $100,000, my approach would certainly have been different, but $5,000 seemed a small price to pay in exchange for a wealth of experience. Best of all, my risk is still paying big dividends for the business, for my employee's company, and for her career.

MANAGERS FROM THE OUTSIDE

Managers with no track record or limited knowledge of the department or operation have the right foundation for bringing out the best in people. This manager is nearly forced to listen and observe—if only for self-preservation.

What You Don't Know Can Hurt You. The new manager is a recruiter's dream: experienced, well-seasoned, an able turnaround leader whose résumé reads like a *Wall Street Journal* fantasy. Still, what he doesn't know could fill a book—and devastate his department.

When Ignorance Goes into Action, Learning Stops. Smart managers have learned to use their ignorance in their favor. Acknowledge your areas of unfamiliarity, and the best way to take charge will make itself obvious; act on them and your ignorance will make itself just as plain.

What the Newly Recruited Outside Manager Does Not Know:

• His or her people. Listen carefully for interpersonal problems or morale difficulties, but reserve judgment for one full month. Don't clean house until you're sure you see the dirt.

"I DON'T KNOW"—ONE OF THE MOST EFFECTIVE YET UNDERUSED STATEMENTS A MANAGER CAN MAKE.

• Details of a subordinate's job. The more certain you are that you can build a better widget than your employees, the greater chances are that you'll be building widgets, not departments.

• Higher management. What you see at an interview is not always what you get. Listen for details that will clue you in to your bosses' preferences and pet peeves before taking action.

• Office procedure. For every action, there is an equal *reaction*. Tamper with office procedure too soon and productivity will give way to confusion or resistance.

The First Week: Basic Training for New Recruits. "The handle of my briefcase hadn't even gotten cold before my employees started filling me in on the departmental problems," one newly recruited traffic manager told me. "My reaction? I checked the train schedule. I didn't want to miss the next one out."

Chances are that if your predecessor had been an effective manager, you would not have been hired. He may have left you a deskful of challenges, but he has also given you the wherewithal to overcome them: your employees.

Forty Hours of Effective Listening. They can reduce your assimilation time by half! Start your new job off right by making your employees partners in the troubleshooting process—and in the success that will follow—and they will rally to your side.

Opening Lines of Communication. The mutual dependency between manager and workers is the basis of an effective communications network. Use your first casual meeting to let your employees know that you need them. Encourage each employee to introduce him- or herself and describe his or her responsibilities; then probe for specific problems with open-ended questions ("How has the turnover rate affected you personally?"). Nowhere are the difficulties of the department more deeply felt than within the ranks. Assure your employees that for every group problem there is a group solution, and you'll inspire team spirit while beginning your troubleshooting campaign.

Ask for Input.   If you arrive at policy changes uni-laterally, you may find yourself on a one-person team. Take ten minutes to explain your challenges to the group ("As you know, this department has been among the hardest hit by the turnover problem."). Then ask for input on any policy changes you may be considering ("Do you feel that appointing an employee mediator as a bridge between upper management and our department will help to in-crease job satisfaction?"). Listen for suggestions and don't be surprised when you learn just how much you do not know.

Admit Your Shortcomings.   It will take your em-ployees less time to assess the extent of your knowledge than it will take you to evaluate theirs. Profess more knowledge than you have, and the respect and confidence of your employees will blow away in the bluster; bluff and you invite testing.

"I Don't Know."   One of the most effective—and underused—statements a manager can make. Say those three little words and you've maintained your credibility; follow them with a positive, reassuring invitation ("Why don't we see if we can find the answer together?") and you've strengthened the bond between you and your subordinates.

FROM RECRUIT TO MANAGER:
AN EIGHT-POINT PLAN

1. When you've begun to learn how much you don't know, admit your ignorance and ask for help.

2. Abstain from making continued comparisons between your old company and your present employer. You may convince some valued employees that the grass really is greener elsewhere.

3. Make your new subordinates feel that their input is critical to their performance and *yours*.

4. Do not create the impression that this job is just a stopping-off point on the way to the top. Employees thrive on a feeling of permanence.

5. Do not make promises that you will not be able to keep.

6. Be objective and reserved in your evaluation of your employees. Some are good workers; others are good actors.

7. Never criticize another supervisor, manager, or employee on a poor decision or performance. Unless you have all the facts, you could just be creating an unnecessary contest.

8. LISTEN—get to know your subordinates and you will get to know your job.

Treat Successes and Failures with an "Ours" Versus "Yours" Attitude. Show appreciation for an individual job well done, but be sure to recognize the importance of the team. Share the good feeling that comes with success and you'll feel it multiply; divide the feelings of frustration that come with failure and they will diminish.

GIVE CREDIT WHERE CREDIT
IS DUE AND YOUR
EMPLOYEES WILL RETURN
THE FAVOR WITH INTEREST.

13

Listening— the Silent Management Tool for Establishing Accountability

**Who is Responsible for Your Employees'
Irresponsibility?
A Manager's Quiz**

Answer yes or no:

1. My employees weren't hired to be self-starters;
they are a task-oriented group.
2. I am the department's sole troubleshooter.
3. When production is down, it is the employee who
should be reprimanded.
4. An employee who does not follow directions without questions is an insubordinate employee.
5. The suggestion box is the mark of a weak, un-
focused manager.

THE REWARDS OF
WORKING SHOULDN'T
JUST FIT INTO A
WALLET; THEY SHOULD
ENRICH THE EGO AS WELL.

This quiz is proof that the truth hurts. The more often you responded true to the above questions, the more likely it is that your employees are not contributing to the work environment; that their productivity is not what it could be; and that *you* may be more of a hindrance than a help.

You Get Back What You Put In.   Offer an employee a job whose rewards can fit into a wallet and he will give you the labor of his hands in return; offer a worker a job whose rewards enrich the self-esteem and she will give you her hands, her mind, and her heart.

Response—the Root of Responsibility.   The confidence to take pride in one's work does not come in a pay envelope; only a manager's positive response can make the difference between a job done and a job *well* done. Withhold response and you withhold the employee's opportunity to take responsibility; offer it freely and you may turn a job into a satisfying career.

Sending the Right Messages.   How many of the following productivity-boosting responses are part of your managerial repertoire?

• "How do you feel we should approach the problem?" Invite the employee to voice his opinions and you invite him to broaden his scope—and to accept responsibility. The worker is assured that his value extends beyond the limits of his labor; yet, he will use his on-the-job skills to see to it that his input is proven correct.

• "Will you follow through on this, please?" Give an employee the opportunity to make a project "his baby," and then watch his dust! Invest your trust in a skilled employee, and he'll do anything rather than let you down.

THE CONFIDENCE
TO TAKE PRIDE IN
ONE'S WORK DOESN'T
COME IN A PAY ENVELOPE.

• "Mary, you've had some experience with the older machines. Do you feel that replacing them would improve our output?" The key to responsibility is involvement. Make your employees partners in your company's future, and they will invest their futures in *you*.

• "Great idea, Sue. Let's give it a try." It is said that genius is one part inspiration and nine parts perspiration. Reward the notion and you'll get the motion—and the instant accountability of the employee.

Are You an Accountability Buster?   If any of these destructive messages seem all too familiar, chances are that you are the root of your own productivity problem:

• "Well, what would you have done instead?" Ask for the opinions of your staff *after* your unilateral plan has failed, and you've set up an intelligence contest between you and your employees. Can you really expect suggestions to flow when each opinion is a blow to your ego?

• "I've decided to . . ." When a one-woman plan fails, it's one woman's problem. By cutting your employees out of your decision-making process, you've excused them from accountability.

• "In my experience . . ." Any manager who shrugs off the suggestions of his employees by pulling rank had better have the voluminous experience he boasts of; he'll need it!

ELIMINATING "WE CAN'T": A SEVEN-POINT PLAN

1. A ready answer for "we can't" is "why not?"

2. Make it known that "we can't" is unacceptable as a final answer to a problem or an opportunity.

3. Encourage a collective thinking process that is focused on creative and imaginative alternatives.

4. Treat problems as challenges that must be overcome.

5. Be positive that a solution is available to any problem.

6. Send this message to your subordinates: That which is yet to be done for the first time is never impossible.

7. Because something was tried and failed does not make it impossible.

14

Effective Listening Means Never Having to Hear "We Can't"

Variations on a Theme. "We tried it before and it didn't work." "I don't think we have the resources to back up a plan of that scope." "What would you say the margin for error is on this thing, anyway?"

No matter how you say it, the meaning remains the same: "We can't." Repeat this negative message often enough and it will become a self-fulfilling—and self-defeating—prophecy.

The Power of Negative Thinking. "We can't"—it's a message that has almost become a dismal mantra. Everywhere I've gone, from the centuries-old factories of the East Coast to the offices along San Francisco Bay, I've heard it echoed daily—by workers, by supervisors, even by general managers. Is any workplace immune from the power of negative thinking? I'd like to think so—because in every department I've ever managed, I've made an effort to "outplace" impossibility.

"WE CAN'T"—OUR
EXCUSE TO STOP THINKING.

"We Can't"—the Big Business Cop-Out.   Why is "we can't" an unacceptable response to a problem or an opportunity? Because it is a lie—worse, it is an easy lie, a lie that comes almost as automatically as breathing. It is our knee-jerk response to an innovative program that might mean work for our department; it is our way of derailing any competitive manager whose train of thought seems to be trespassing on our territory; most damaging of all, it is our excuse, as managers or workers, to stop thinking.

What Happens When We Say "We Can."   When we begin to view the realm of "impossibility" as unexplored territory, our life maps and career goals can double in size and scope. Our thinking becomes focused on "how we *can*"; and our energies, no longer needed for excuse-making, are channeled in a more positive direction.

Positive Management.   No employee really wants to accept "I can't" as his or her credo. The limitations are stifling, the potential for growth nearly nil. Yet, employees can become trapped by the easy lie, particularly if led by a "can't do" manager. Use these guidelines to break the grip of negativity, freeing your valued employees to think creatively, judge objectively, and make the "impossible" a profitable reality:

• Try and try again. "We have tried that before and it didn't work." Negative statements rooted in company history (a history you may not share) not only keep the employee from progressing, but can foster a feeling of hopelessness throughout the firm. Focus on the positive by probing with questions like this: "What steps would you take, then, to ensure a more successful outcome?" The employee is forced to consider the possibilities and to put preconceived "impossibilities" aside.

GENIUS IS THE
ABILITY TO BREAK
THE BOUNDS OF
MUNDANE THINKING.

• Accentuate the positive. Taking a negative approach to a problem is like taking a detour: You may eventually get where you're going, but you go miles out of your way.

As the newly recruited manager of a large sales force, it was my job to find out why morale—and sales—had been slipping. I found the answer in the least likely of places—in my top desk drawer. That salespeople are obligated to fill out a report form after each call is, in most organizations, business as usual; yet the forms I discovered were so negative that I was convinced they were at the root of some of the department's problems.

"Business Lost—Why?" That was the one heading that had been allotted the greatest amount of space on the report, and as far as I could see, all of that space was wasted space. It was an invitation for the employee to cover his tail, to provide his manager with excuses rather than positive input. And when I leafed through the reports filed by my staff in the last month, my assessment was confirmed. One after another, each of the forms had been completed with this simple, profound message—"we can't."

My response was twofold: first, to hold an open, casual meeting on the subject of *possibility*; then, to call the printer. In less than a week, "Business Lost—Why?" had been replaced by "Steps Taken to Recoup Lost Business," both on the form and in the minds of my employees. And that's when business began to pick up.

A Shot in the Arm.   Find an operation that has been having managerial problems, sales, production, or processing difficulties and you have found a group of people who have been poisoned by the power of negative thinking. Although it is the manager's responsibility to diagnose departmental problems, any prolonged group discussion of the tribulations only reinforces the negative symptoms. As soon as you have a handle on the nature of the disease, focus your attention on the cure. Encourage your people to think positively, to seek out solutions rather than wallow in negativity, and even the most troubled department will soon be on the mend.

From the Ridiculous to the Sublime.   Genius is the ability to break the bounds of mundane thinking. To make this method of management work, you must be prepared to entertain all types of suggestions, from the logical to the ludicrous. Yet, the more you listen, the less likely you will be listening to the big business cop-out: "We can't."

15

Listening—the Mother of Innovation

The manager who listens effectively, responds positively, and encourages subordinates to think independently creates an atmosphere that fosters creativity. Nourish and channel the seeds of creativity and employee inventiveness will grow; focus inventiveness and innovation takes root.

NOURISHING CREATIVITY

"If only I could harness the creative efforts that go into my salespeople's expense reports and focus them on selling, we could increase our sales by twenty-five percent!" It's an old sales manager's joke, and I could tell by the old sales manager's response that *he* felt it was funny. What wasn't so funny was that, in a single one-liner, he had effectively pinpointed himself as the cause of his department's problems. He knew that his people had the capacity to be creative, but he wasn't about to lift a finger in focusing or nurturing that spark of genius.

Creativity Needs Tending. Inventiveness untrained soon becomes untrainable. Creativity unappreciated will

NOURISH AND CHANNEL
THE SEEDS OF
CREATIVITY, AND
EMPLOYEE INVENTIVENESS
WILL GROW.

CONSTRUCTIVE CRITICISM
WELL RECEIVED WILL
SOON TURN TO PRAISE.

never take root. Innovation ignored goes to seed. But cultivate a climate of mutual supportiveness, and ideas—and morale—will flourish.

Good Ideas: Building Blocks of Great Ideas. Fran, the customer service representative, was proud of her innovation: Her new procedure enabling the organization to contact customers through telecommunications was bound to make a big impact on the department. She would have been satisfied with providing a good idea until her manager encouraged her to make it a *great* one.

"Super idea, Fran. Do you think we might be able to apply that solution to any other aspects of the business?" That challenge was all Fran needed to hear. Shortly thereafter, her expanded good idea made its way to the corner office—and now Fran is sitting in an office of her own.

Brainstorming: An Exercise in Mass Creativity. Break down any insecurities your employees may have about offering their creative input by holding a brief, casual departmental brainstorming session. Take a moment to introduce the problem; then sit back and let those creative juices flow! Demonstrate your interest and your willingness to accept *all* suggestions (no matter how impractical) by logging them in as they are offered. Interject only to keep the meeting focused and to probe with open-ended questions, and you've opened the door to communication—and opened your employees' minds to creative thought.

Be Critical, Not Hypocritical. Although a manager is obligated to stimulate creativity, he or she is also responsible for disciplining employees' urges for innovation. Inventiveness untrained soon becomes untrainable; creative suggestions left uncriticized yet untried can frustrate subordinates into keeping their ideas to themselves.

The road to constructive criticism is really just a very

THE SEVEREST CRITIC IS ONE
WHO IS TOTALLY INDIFFERENT.

thin line. Whether you kill the creative urge with false kindness or smother it with negativity, a step in the wrong direction can render innovation a dead issue.

When an Employee's Idea Has Missed Its Mark, Check the Target. Were your needs ever made clear? A nonjudgmental statement such as "Maybe I didn't explain enough of the details on the project" opens up the lines of communication. Follow with an open-ended question such as "What is your perception of what I was looking for in a new data-processing system?" and you'll soon get to the root of any communication problem.

Accentuate the Positive. If the employee's suggestion is simply impractical or shortsighted, begin your critique with a sincere compliment ("Your evaluation of the problem as a whole was right on target!"), then follow with a nonconfrontational, *objective* analysis of the error ("But I think we need to take a closer look at section two and its impact on operations.").

Remember, constructive criticism is a focusing tool. Use it intelligently and sensitively, and your employees will feel directed. Aim it like a weapon and it will backfire.

LETTERS ARE OFTEN
USED TO HELP US
SEE WHAT WE
COULDN'T HEAR.

16

Listening to Written Communication

Effective listening not only means decoding verbal signals; it means tuning in to written communication as well. Although it helps to know the background and personality of the correspondent, some key elements of written communication can clue you in to the messages in—and between—the lines.

Reading Between the Lines: A Manager's Quiz

Read the following letter carefully. (Do not turn the page when you've finished.) Then, on a separate piece of paper write the main point that Mr. Johnson is attempting to communicate to Ms. Davis.

WHAT IS THE LETTER REALLY SAYING? "I STILL WANT TO DO BUSINESS WITH YOUR COMPANY."

Alice Davis, President

Good Folding Box Company

Dear Ms. Davis:

I regret to inform you that we will have to terminate your company as a vendor due to your poor reaction to our needs over the past year. We feel that your broker, Bob Smith, has done a good job in working with us, but his calls and letters to your home office have not produced the necessary results.

We regret having to make this decision. Ours has been a long and, for the most part, productive working relationship. However, we trust that you recognize that, in the perishables market, service and delivery are of paramount importance.

Sincerely,

Chuck Johnson,

Purchasing Manager

CREATIVE FLOWERS, INC.

What is Chuck Johnson really saying to the Good Folding Box Company? "I still want to do business with your company."

The Message Behind Every Business Letter. "I care about our working relationship." A client or customer who does not care is not a client or customer who takes the time to write.

Chuck Johnson's letter should have signaled that the Good Folding Box Company still fills a need for Creative Flowers, Inc. The relatively cordial "I regret to inform you" is a genuine statement of disappointment, yet, "Bob Smith has done a good job in working with us" tempers the reprimand. But it is the final sentence that is the key: "We

LETTERS ARE OFTEN
A SYMPTOM OF A
MORE DEEPLY ROOTED
PROBLEM OR CONCERN.

trust that you recognize that, in the perishables market, service and delivery are of paramount importance" is a reminder of Creative Flowers' needs—a reminder that would hardly be necessary if the relationship were truly being severed.

A Letter Is Often a Symptom of a More Deeply Rooted Problem. What if Good Folding Box really had been a poor vendor? Then, a sharp Ms. Davis might wonder *why* Creative Flowers still wants to do business. If her company's prices are the attraction, are they too low? Is the broker too close to the account? Is Johnson attempting a price squeeze?

Don't overlook any messages you find between the lines. What remains to be said *must* be read.

One must be cautious in analyzing written communication because it presents one special circumstance that does not exist in verbal communication: You cannot see or be sure who has done the actual writing. Letters may be composed by individuals other than those who sign them, or they may be used as a hiding place for the "masked messenger."

The Masked Messenger. When a client or customer's written communication does not ring true, chances are that his or her letter has been dictated by a superior, or a "masked messenger." The emergence of a third party in what had been a two-party line of communication *always* signals danger. Your contact may be on the verge of outplacement, your business agreements may be in jeopardy, or your contact's superiors may be reassessing *your* abilities.

Unmask any MMs before they sneak up on you by watching for these correspondence clues:

• The use of terminology unknown or unused by your contact.

NO MATTER WHAT
YOUR INTENDED MESSAGE,
PUTTING IT IN WRITING
SAYS THAT YOU CARE.

• A formal salutation. (A "Dear John" letter takes on even more dire consequences when it's addressed to "Dear Mr. Smythe.")

• The inclusion of *any* legal terminology (a sure sign that the company's counsel is the masked messenger).

• The insistence that you respond in writing rather than in person or by telephone.

• Any letter from a contact or client who normally relies on the telephone as a communication tool.

Last-Attempt Letters.   Although every letter sends a message that it's time to sit down and listen, the "last-attempt" missive is an unmistakable signal that you have turned a deaf ear to a valuable client. Following are two kinds of last attempts. Most of us would probably like to believe that these examples differ significantly (business school *must* count for something!), but the fact is that both letters communicate the same simple message: "You aren't listening to me."

> My first attempt to reach you, on January 5, was foiled by your secretary. Although I was assured that she would certainly alert you to the urgency of the matter, when I had not heard from you by noon the next day, I phoned again, only to be told that you were "in conference."
> As you recall, I placed my order with you in the understanding that delivery would be made no later than January 2. Your silence on the matter, and the tardiness of the shipment, indicate to me that your interest in Weldon Manufacturing does not extend beyond the limits of your accounts receivable department. Therefore, I cancel my order and request that you remit $4,375, the amount of my payment, within the next 30 days.

ANY "LAST-ATTEMPT" LETTER MUST BECOME YOUR FIRST PRIORITY.

DEAR MOM,
   IF YOU DON'T
   LET ME PLAY WitH
   MY bEST FrEND TiMMY,
   I WiLL RUN AWAY.
                    JIMMY

Making the Last Attempt Your First Priority. A client who has been forced to demand attention is a client who has been forced to acknowledge that he or she is no longer important to you.

Making restitution may not be easy (or even possible), but it is never too late to listen—and learn. Make the last attempt your first priority. At best, you will win back your client's confidence; at worst, you will go your way a little wiser. Remember these points:

• Respond to the last attempt letter immediately, in person or by phone. Delay communication and you confirm your client's worst suspicions.

• Don't make excuses! Mitigating factors may have prevented you from fulfilling your responsibilities, but what prevented you from reporting these unexpected circumstances? There is no excuse for a lack of communication.

• Focus on the positive. Ask the client what you can do to make up for the inconvenience you have caused—then go the distance to ensure his or her satisfaction.

WHEN YOU TALK TOO MUCH,
IT IS JUST AS HARD TO
REMEMBER ALL THAT YOU
SAID AS IT IS TO REMEMBER
WHAT IT IS THEY SAID.

• Listen—without interruption—until the client feels you have heard the whole story. Then,

• Follow up the phone call in writing. No matter what its content, a letter's underlying message is "I care." Recommit to your mutual dependency by taking the time to put your solutions in writing.

EVALUATE THE IMPORTANCE
OF THE SUBJECT TO
THE OTHER INDIVIDUAL;
WHAT IS INSIGNIFICANT
TO YOU MAY BE OF
UTMOST IMPORTANCE
TO THAT PERSON.

17

Listening and the Manager's Meeting

Are You Tuned In at the Conference Table?
A Manager's Quiz

Take this quiz within three hours after your next manager's meeting. Answer yes or no:

1. You left the meeting feeling empty. Even now, you wonder what you said.
2. You entered the meeting not knowing its objective.
3. You know little more now than you did before the meeting.
4. Since the meeting, you have contacted other employees to clarify what transpired.
5. You wonder how other managers feel about the outcome of the meeting.
6. You feel that another meeting is necessary to fully clarify this one.
7. Think back to the last time an employee asked you for information on a recent policy change. Could you answer his or her questions?

TOO MANY MEETINGS
ARE A CLEAR SIGNAL
THAT A COMPANY
IS IN TROUBLE.

Each yes you answered to the first six questions means that you are cheating yourself by tuning out at the conference table. If you answered no to question 7, your inability to listen to your peers is cheating your subordinates out of the benefits of having a fully engaged manager.

A Road Map Is Useless Unless You Know Where You Are Going. Effective listening is your best road map. Tune in to the signals in your workplace, and you will be prepared for any sharp turns, unexpected twists, or unpredictable drops in your business, in your career, and in your dealings with your subordinates. But where are you going?

The Manager's Meeting: A Full-Service Stopoff. Pass it by and business trends will soon pass *you* by. Steer in with your listening apparatus fully engaged and you'll tune your focus. The manager's meeting is your chance to get your foot off the accelerator, and:

• Refuel—to set new objectives that stimulate you, to feed off the bond between you and your colleagues.

• Ask for directions—to focus your attention on the road ahead and to evaluate objectively what's behind you.

• Make repairs—on the problems that are slowing your department down as well as those that affect the direction of the entire company; check the timing of new programs or policies; and reinforce common goals.

WHEN THE RESULT OF
A MEETING IS TO SCHEDULE
MORE MEETINGS,
YOU NEED TO ASSESS
IF YOUR MEETINGS
ARE A CRUTCH FOR
INEFFECTIVE MANAGEMENT.

GEARING UP FOR THE MANAGER'S MEETING: A FIVE-POINT PLAN

Follow these guidelines and you'll get the most out of your management team meetings:

1. Schedule not only the meeting time, but its objective, into your work week. Everyone listens more effectively when he or she knows what to listen *for.* Record the goal of the meeting in your planner and you'll enhance the possibility of reaching it.

2. Put your opinions on the objective in writing. Meetings can mean pressure, and anxiety can obliterate the memory. Make notes on what you plan to say, and as the meeting progresses, record any reactions to your suggestions. Chronicling the workings—and the failings—of your management team will give you a handle on the company's needs and a perspective on individual personalities.

3. Listen for negativity. The management team stops making progress and starts wasting time the instant the problems become more important than the solutions. One positive question or comment from you ("What do you feel my department can contribute to alleviate the problem, John?") realigns focus and saves time.

4. Listen for finger-pointing. Let an issue become a "hot potato" and the futile pass-the-blame game begins. Defuse this potentially explosive situation by rallying the team: "If shipments have been late, Nancy, then it's a company problem, not a departmental problem."

5. Respond. Remain silent and allow decisions to be made for you, and you have handed your department's future to a more vociferous manager, who may be only too glad to make your decisions for you. Response is the root of responsibility! Support the interests of your subordinates and they will support you.

Do You Spend Too Much Time in Meetings?
A Manager's Quiz

Answer yes or no:

1. Is more than ten percent of your work week spent in meetings?
2. Is it a common practice to come out of one meeting with a schedule for two more meetings?
3. Do departmental or planning meetings take precedence over visiting a customer?
4. Does your spouse or do your friends ever say "It seems like all you do is go to meetings"?
5. Do you have a set schedule of meetings each week even if there's no agenda?
6. Is your first reaction to a problem "Let's call a meeting"?

If you responded yes to any of the above questions, *you* may be using meetings as a crutch.

The president of a multimillion-dollar plastics corporation asked for my recommendations after studying the poor performance of one of his divisions. My simple answer to all of his problems? No more weekly executive committee meetings! The conferences, once a constructive forum for providing direction, had become nothing more than a finger-pointing session where the company's problems were being assessed for *blame* rather than corrective action. My "no meetings" dictum forced the president to direct—on his own—and the managers to manage without a crutch. Soon the company was walking tall in the market again simply because its staff had resumed the duties they were hired to perform.

Too many meetings are often a sign of indecisive management, overstaffing, and lack of concrete direction.

Use these strategies to keep yours to a constructive minimum:

• Never schedule meetings by the calendar. Schedule them by *need*. The "if-it's-Monday-I-must-be-in-a-meeting" mentality makes your conferences seem like a chore, not a tool.

• Before scheduling a meeting, ask yourself the following questions: Is this meeting an excuse to diffuse the responsibility for my decisions? Do I have a planned agenda? Is this a matter that can be resolved as easily with one-on-one communication?

• Think of all the things you—and your staff—could be doing instead of attending the meeting you plan. Is the conference really more important than those responsibilities?

WHEN THE ABSENCE OF
COMMUNICATION BETWEEN
A MANAGER AND A
SUBORDINATE CREATES
A VOID, MISUNDERSTANDING
CAN SOON FILL THAT VOID.

18

Listening Exercises for the Manager

What Difference Does a Day Make? For three consecutive days, skim the Bible of the business world, *The Wall Street Journal.* Even the most cursory reading will tell you that the difference between one business day and the next is the difference between a merger and a buy-out, between a bankruptcy and an unprecedented profit— between success and failure. Now, stop to consider that each of those upturns and downswings is the result of people working effectively—or ineffectively—together, and each day in your department will begin to take on its true meaning.

Give Each Day Its Due. This means accepting the following theorem as the basis of your management plan: Nothing is certain but change.

Take a few moments each day to tap in to your employees' needs and objectives, and you tap in to the power of positive change; learn to listen to their sound solutions and creative innovations, and turn every new day

**TREAT EMPLOYEES LIKE
MACHINES AND YOU CAN
EXPECT A BREAKDOWN—
IN COMMUNICATION
AND IN MORALE.**

into a new opportunity. What difference can a day make? Put effective listening to work for you today and you'll always be ready for tomorrow.

Talk to Each Direct Report at Least Once a Day. When the absence of communication between a manager and a subordinate creates a void, misunderstanding will soon fill that void.

Remember that the manager is one of the most important people in the employee's life. Making yourself available assures the employee that you accept the responsibilities of that role. It also communicates your interest and creates a feeling of involvement.

There is no greater barrier to communication than distance; take the first step and your employees will meet you halfway.

Keep Up-to-Date on the First Names, Last Names, and Nicknames of Each Worker in Your Department. Address your subordinates by name and you say "I care." Allow your employees to address *you* by name and you say "I want *you* to care along with me."

What's in a name? Recognition, encouragement, and warmth. Open every conversation with a personal address and you open the lines of honest communication.

Note Important Dates in the Lives of Your Subordinates. Several years ago, when I was employed at a large food company, an associate was suddenly summoned to the president's office. Having had limited contact with the president before, she was filled with apprehension—could an error of hers have traveled *that* far? Would she be cornered in the corner office?

Imagine her relief when the president offered his hand (instead of the boot) to congratulate her on the ten-year anniversary of her employment! The fact that the president knew of her decade of service was impressive enough, but that he took the time to thank her personally established a

ENTHUSIASM IS WHAT
KEEPS YOU HEADING FOR
THE LONG-RANGE GOALS
DESPITE THE HURDLES OF
THE SHORT-RANGE FAILURES.

bond of loyalty that is still strong today—more than five years later.

Take the time to acknowledge life's events—like birthdays and service anniversaries—and you let your employees know that you value their humanity as well as their skills. Treat them like machines and you can expect a breakdown—in communication and in morale.

Press Your Lips Together At Least Twice a Day to Avoid Talking When You Should Be Listening. Caution! This exercise may cause a temporary deflation of your ego—but the lift it will give to morale and productivity will be permanent!

Even the smallest investment in an employee's self-esteem will pay big dividends in accountability and confidence. Your people are your greatest resource. Pay them the ultimate compliment: *Listen.*

Laugh at Yourself at Least Once a Day. Yes, in public! You are human, too. It will come as no surprise to your employees that the more you try to accomplish, the greater your possibility of error.

Take the time to laugh at your errors with your subordinates and you encourage them to come forward with their own suggestions. By listening to their feedback concerning your decisions, you assure them that you are not above reproach.

Laughter is the voice of enthusiasm, and enthusiasm is what keeps you heading for the long-range goals despite the hurdles of short-range failures.

And When All Else Fails, Look in the Mirror. Nature provided you with two ears but only one mouth. Are you listening twice as often as you're talking?

MONEY TALKS!
How to get it and How to keep it!

Now, for the first time in paperback
The Record-Breaking #1 Bestseller
with over 2.6 million hardcover copies sold
Iacocca: An Autobiography
by Lee Iacocca with William Novak
☐ (25147-3 • $4.95)

He's an American legend, the tough-talking, straight-shooting businessman who brought Chrysler back from the brink of financial doom and in the process became a media celebrity and a newsmaker. He's the son of Italian immigrants who rose spectacularly through the ranks of the Ford Motor Company to become its president, only to be knocked down eight years later in a devastating power play. He's the man who got even by transforming a floundering Chrysler Corporation into a booming success, leading a fight for survival that has become legendary.

Now the record-breaking hardcover bestseller is available in paperback: Lee Iacocca's life in his own words.

Now in Trade Paperback
the #1 National Bestseller
What They Don't Teach You at Harvard Business School
Notes From a Street-Smart Executive
☐ by Mark H. McCormack
(34583 • $9.95)

Over 500,000 hardcover copies were sold of this straight-talking advice from one of the most successful entrepreneurs in American business. Based on his proven method of *applied people sense* to get things done, McCormack's street-smart advice offers insights into how to read people and yourself, sales negotiation and executive time management. This is a "must-read" for executives at every level.